My Appalachian Trail

H. DALE HALL

My Appalachian Trail
H. Dale Hall
Published May 2023
Heirloom Editions
Imprint of Jan-Carol Publishing, Inc.
All rights reserved
Copyright © 2023 H. Dale Hall

This book may not be reproduced in whole or part, in any manner whatsoever, without written permission, with the exception of brief quotations within book reviews or articles.

ISBN: 978-1-954978-88-1
Library of Congress Control Number: 2023938049

You may contact the publisher:
Jan-Carol Publishing, Inc.
PO Box 701
Johnson City, TN 37605
publisher@jancarolpublishing.com
www.jancarolpublishing.com

*This book is dedicated to
Rubin and Callie Colwell, Milton and Joanna Hall,
Herbert and Frances Hall, Herman and Nell Reed,
Sarah, Erin, Adam, Emily, and all the heirs of this wonderful family,
that they may appreciate their rich Appalachian and Cajun history.*

And to all the hearty pioneers that settled eastern Kentucky.

PHOTO BY DR. HOMER FORTNEY

Harlan, Kentucky

AUTHOR'S NOTE

The Cumberland Plateau of the Appalachian Mountains in eastern Kentucky is one of the most beautiful places on Earth. The peaks and valleys have been home to Native American and immigrant people for centuries, people who simply sought the opportunity to work hard, raise children, and live in peace with the bounty the Creator has given.

I was blessed to be born and raised in Harlan County by a loving mother and father with caring family on both the Harlan and Leslie County branches of the family. While we were poor by standards of economics, we were wealthy in the things that really matter in life. My journey from Harlan County to meetings in the halls of the White House was cocooned with those important teachings, and I never left those beautiful hills and the people that live there behind. Their love was always with me. Many outsiders believe hill poverty breeds hopelessness and despair. I beg to differ. I hope this book helps you feel the hope, determination, richness, and warmth of the wonderful hill culture that is Appalachian.

CHAPTER 1:
The Deliverance

He was gently laying on his side, looking at the sky and wondering how long he had been there. He remembered seeing a magnificent night sky with what seemed to be a million stars in the Milky Way. Or had he dreamed it? The South Pacific climate provided the island of Los Negros in Papua New Guinea with constant temperatures between 70 and 85 degrees throughout the year, except for the monsoons from December through February. It was early March 1944, and he was spared the additional challenges of torrential rain in the jungle where he had concealed himself. He had been in and out of consciousness repeatedly and could smell dried blood and the residue of gun powder in his clothes from the battle. All sense of time had been lost as he tried to focus on staying alive.

A Japanese hand grenade had done its job and left a piece of shrapnel in his chest. Troop H, 5th Cavalry, unknowingly left him behind and moved forward in pursuit of the enemy. It was up to him to keep himself alive any way he could. He did as he had been taught in his survival training and applied direct pressure to the wound to stop the bleeding. This wound, however, was not a small bullet hole that could be plugged with a finger. He placed his index, middle, and ring fingers as tightly together as he could and forced them into the gash left by the hot metal that remained embedded in his chest. He could feel the sharp, splintery edges of his rib cage as he pushed to stop the bleeding. Adrenaline and endorphins were aiding in subduing the pain, but it was small relief from the trauma his body was fighting.

The battle was late in the afternoon as they were pushing through the dense understory where the enemy had ample opportunities to be concealed. The flash of light and the burning sensation in his chest caused him to be stunned and in horrendous pain. The explosion temporarily deafened him. He was in a daze but knew the bleeding was serious and needed to be stopped quickly. He didn't want to die in this godforsaken jungle where headhunters and cannibals still lived. He wanted to see his home in the hills of Harlan County Kentucky and raise a family there, just as his ancestors had done before him. He had to survive!

Herbert Hall was born in Elcomb, Kentucky in Harlan County to Milton Hall and Joanna Forester. He was the eighth of eleven children, not an uncommon number in the early 1900s when children were needed to work the garden and help with the chores. Milt was born in 1878 and Joanna in 1885, both in Harlan, and were married in 1905. They began their family with the birth of Nannie in 1906, followed by Dezzie, Elbert, Verna, Lee, Mary, Pearl, Herbert (1917), Hubert, Robert, and Nell. Herb and his brothers had more than one fight with other boys when they were growing up by being teased as the "Bert Brothers." Milt and Joanna also didn't see fit to give Herb a middle name or initial, so the Army called him Herbert "NMI" Hall: No Middle Initial.

Milton Hall and Joanna Forester Hall, 1905

Scratching out a living in the Elcomb bottoms was not an easy task in the early 1900s. Milt walked the railroad tracks to the Mary Helen coal mines each day, and the kids made the five-mile trek to the Beach Grove School. Joanna lived the life of a pioneer woman in Appalachia, where over 450 million years ago the tectonic plates and receding glaciers combined to carve out the mountains and hollows of eastern Kentucky. The mountains were beautiful with oaks, elms, mountain mahogany, and mountain chestnut, but often so close together it made her feel as if she were in the folds of an accordion. In each hollow was a "bottom," or flat area where the stream would swell each spring with flood waters. Some areas between the hills were as little as one hundred yards, while others could reach a mile and allow farming to take place after the rich alluvium of the flood had been deposited.

Harlan was the County seat and only a few miles away, which gave more access to the basic necessities not normally available to the majority of hill people. The only real opportunities for work were the coal mines and the railroad to haul the coal out. Other occupations were almost completely in support of mining, and the mine operators were the Kentucky equivalent of overlords. Milt and Joanna made their lives at the "Old Home Place," the homestead of Milt's father and mother (Britton Hall and Nancy Ledford), which gave them slightly more autonomy from the grip of the mine operators. The railroad hugged the hillside as it ran through the bottom and provided a walkway to their small country church on Sunday. Herb had grown up in the safe environment of family as neighbors, but also developed a strong aversion to working in the mines. Whether he didn't care for the prospect of spending 12 to 14 hours a day in a deep hole with only one way out or his desire to go out into the world and find a better trade was never revealed, he knew he didn't want to work in the mines.

By the 1920s, things were going good in Harlan. The "roaring twenties" were underway and the nation needed coal. It's difficult to say what causes someone to feel overcome by the stresses of raising eleven children and tending to the cooking and cleaning, but at some point, it snapped for Joanna. In 1929, she came to believe that Milt was seeing another woman. There is no evidence to either prove or disprove the allegation, but it didn't matter. Joanna believed it. On June 20, 1929, Joanna Forester Hall stood on her front porch with 9-year-old Hubert playing nearby and swallowed a lethal dose of strychnine (Lee 2019). Strychnine was a common drug for many ailments in the late 19th and early 20th centuries and was easily obtainable. Hill people were very protective of family matters and reluctant to share private information. What happened in a family was nobody else's business and there would be no cause for gossip and whispering. The obituary for Joanna stated she died "due to high blood pressure." Milt never remarried.

Jackie Goshen Lee said, "After Joanna's death, Nannie and Lee were the oldest girls and did all the cooking and taking care of the house. They stole chickens and did whatever they could to keep everybody fed." Herb was eleven at the time and a boy who loved to play and get in trouble. Years later, he would chuckle while listening to Cawood Ledford, the voice of the University of Kentucky sports for decades, call a game on the radio: "I hit Cawood right in the eye with a rock during a rock fight when we were kids. Now look where he is!" Ledford was inducted into the National Sports Media Hall of Fame in 2020, more than 18 years after his death. Herb was a rounder and had a temper, but it is also likely that this stubborn temperament helped him survive the challenge of being wounded in battle.

In the boom years, a lot of people came to Harlan looking for work in the mines. For those that didn't have roots there or an "Old Home Place," the miners and their families lived in company camps in houses supplied by the mine owners and were often paid in "script" instead of money. The script was only good at the company stores. This monopoly over the lives of miners made them the equivalent of indentured servants. The extremely modest houses they lived in were owned by the mine, all purchases were made at the company store with script or on credit, and the miners had no recourse but to run up a credit bill. Miners were paid by the ton of coal they produced, usually a few cents a ton. Tennessee Ernie Ford released a song in 1947 with the lyrics:

> "You load sixteen tons and what do you get?
> Another day older and deeper in debt.
> Saint Peter don't you call me 'cause I can't go,
> I owe my soul to the company store."

For the miners, there wasn't any real hope for a future. Children were forced to work alongside adults to help families meet their needs. In the midst of the Great Depression, the coal industry made a significant push to have coal be the nation's energy source. They reduced the price of coal to encourage a national move and cut the wages of miners by 10% to make up the difference. Eventually the miners had enough, and the emotional breakpoint arrived when the United Mine Workers of America and, to a smaller extent, the National Miners' Union came into Harlan to encourage them to organize for collective bargaining. Needless to say, the coal operators fought this "infiltration of outsiders" with all they had; and they had a lot.

The police were bought and paid for by the mine operators, and the miners were seen as nothing more than unskilled labor that should be "happy they have jobs." After all, it was the operators who had made the financial investments and bought (in some cases, stole) the rights to the coal for pennies on the dollar from landowners who had no idea what the coal was worth. It was *their* property. The miners felt they had no recourse but to join the Union and go on strike. That's when Harlan County Kentucky became known as "Bloody Harlan."

The lines were drawn, and the killing lasted from 1931 to 1939. In my college political science class, I was stunned to read in the textbook that in 1939, there were more reported murders in Harlan County, Kentucky than in the British Isles. It was common for a striking miner's home to be riddled with gunshots in the middle of the night while his wife and children were sleeping inside. Before the end of the conflict, the Kentucky National Guard was called in to control "the Reds," as the Union organizers were called, a reference to communists. They played this up based on the accusations that the National Miners' Union supported socialism.

The story goes that, in 1931, Florence Reece was sitting at her mine camp home with her children when Harlan County Sheriff J.H. Blair and his deputies barged into her home, ransacking everything and asking where her striking husband had gone. She replied she didn't know. They left her home in shambles. She took a calendar down from the wall and on the back wrote the song "Which Side Are You On?" which became the anthem of coal miners and unionizing across America. It was clear that Bloody Harlan was no place to be without a gun, and Herb Hall had one.

Herb had dropped out of school after completing eighth grade, not an unusual decision at the time. While he didn't look for trouble, he was known to say, "I never intended to start a fight, but I sure intended to be there at the end" (Grizzle 2019). He had many relatives and friends who were walking the picket lines and, therefore, receiving threats or actual violent actions. While he was never part of the strike, there was no doubt which side *he* was on. By the end of the 1930s, Herb was ready to get out of Harlan and away from the killing. There was a lot of the world he wanted to see, and it was time to see it.

Herbert "NMI" Hall joined the Army on January 15, 1941, at the age of 23. He was a man of slight build, five feet seven inches tall, weighing around 135 pounds. He had crystal blue eyes and black wavy hair that attracted many a young girl. Trained as a machine gunner and truck driver, he quickly gained the respect of his fellow soldiers and officers and was made a squad leader. Everything was normal for Herb in a peacetime Army until 326 days after he enlisted. On December 7, 1941, the Japanese attacked Pearl Harbor and the whole world changed. Herb was assigned to the Asiatic-Pacific Theatre of Operations and eventually shipped to Papua New Guinea as part of the Los Negros Campaign.

Clockwise from top left: Hubert, Robert, Herbert (in uniform), and Elbert Hall, 1941

The Admiralty Islands, lying west of the Bismarck Archipelago in the South Pacific, were critically important to the Japanese as a supply line to the islands of New Guinea, New Britain and New Ireland, and to the Americans for the airstrips and harbors. The Japanese had held the islands since the last war and, in his quest to return to the Philippines, General Douglas McArthur deemed it essential that the Japanese supply line be cut off and the Archipelago belong to the Americans. On February 28, 1944, the assault began with troops preparing to land on the beaches, clear the jungle of resistance, and take the Momote Airstrip. On February 29, the beach was secured with little resistance. But as the

American troops advanced towards the airstrip, the Japanese used the cover of the jungle to offer significant resistance. During the next five days, one thousand two hundred and forty Americans were reported killed and thousands more wounded.

The day had begun like all the others with a slight island breeze and chow of K-rations. Troop H started off on patrol into the jungle to find and overcome the Japanese soldiers that were fiercely trying to defend *their* islands. The Japanese had no intention of giving away this prime South Pacific real estate without a fight. The American forces had to contend with snipers in the trees and Japanese hiding in tunnels to ambush with grenades and machine gun fire that could thunder at any moment. It was later in the afternoon that all hell broke loose. Screams of "Take cover!" and "Hit the dirt!" were heard among the thunderous rapid explosions of rifles, grenades, and machine guns. Panic and training kicked in and all senses were in survival mode. The noise was deafening. It was during the unbridled chaos that the shockwave blast and flash of light occurred next to Herb. There is nothing that can prepare you for the assault and pain of something tearing through your chest. As he waited over the next hours with his three fingers firmly planted in the wound, he prayed to God to let him live. Through the night and into the next morning he remained curled in this lifesaving, fetal position.

The sun had been up for a few hours when he heard soldiers approaching. A new wave of panic shot through his body! Were they Japanese? Had he survived all this time only to become a prisoner of war? He had heard the rumors of how the Japanese treated prisoners and how they believed you were not honorable if you allowed yourself to be captured. The Japanese culture made it so honorable to die in battle that Japanese mothers are reported to have given their sons suicide knives as gifts when they departed for combat duty. But then he heard it. English! The beautiful sound of English being spoken! He found enough strength to call for help, and a medic appeared. "This man is still alive! Bring a stretcher!" Herb had been lying in the dense Papua New Guinea jungle, seriously wounded, for seventeen hours with his three fingers of pressure saving his life (Grizzle 2019). He had survived.

The wounded were carried back to Battalion 8 at the Army field hospital, where the techniques for open heart surgery had not yet been developed. The Army surgeons did a miraculous job of patching him back together and preparing him for transportation to a more stable hospital. But they also gave him the news that they could not remove the shrapnel from his chest because it was too close to his heart. More sobering, they predicted he only had about 20 years to live. After being stabilized, he was moved to an Army hospital ship in the harbor. Herb believed God had granted his wish to live and resolved not to waste the time he had left. He was transported back to the United States where he was taken to Thayer General Hospital in Nashville, Tennessee for the remainder of his recuperation. General McArthur made his highly scripted walk onto those same beaches where, by March 14, the Island and airstrip were under American control.

Herb's sister, Lee; her husband, Charlie Goshen; and their daughter, Jackie, went to visit him in the early part of 1944. Jackie remembers as a young girl making the trip to see Herb and sitting outside the Grand Old Opry in a long line in the "bitter cold," waiting to go inside and hear Roy Acuff perform. This was a side benefit of the trip to Nashville few from Harlan could have enjoyed at the time. The war was still underway, and they had to borrow gas rations from friends and family to have enough fuel to make the trip. Herb stayed at Thayer General Hospital until his recovery and release. His discharge papers placed his health condition as "Poor." He was presented the Purple Heart and Honorably Discharged from the Army on November 24, 1944. During his trip back to the states and time in the hospital, he learned that Milt had died of a stroke in 1943.

It is not surprising that the ordeal he went through inflicted mental as well as physical damage. In World War II, it was called "shell shock." Today, we know it as Post Traumatic Stress Disorder (PTSD), and we also better understand that there are varying degrees of distress that remain throughout the rest of their lives. Herb had been deeply affected by the trauma but was one of the fortunate ones who was able to draw on strong will to keep the symptoms under control. But there is no doubt he was haunted by the ordeal for the rest of his life. When he was released from the hospital, he took his $300 mustering out pay and caught a bus to Harlan. After visiting family for a few months and paying respects to the graves of his parents, it was time to start taking advantage of the little time he had left. He caught another bus, this time to Cincinnati.

CHAPTER 2:

The Colwells

Frances Colwell sat on the porch of her modest eastern Kentucky home on the side of a hill in Leslie County. She enjoyed looking across the Middle Fork of the Kentucky River which joined Wilder Branch about a mile downstream, creating the basis for the naming of her hollow community of Confluence. Just up Dry Hill Road towards Hyden, one could cross the river and go up another hollow, Hell for Certain. The "Hell for Certain Baptist Church" may be the most uniquely named house of prayer one could possibly find. Hyden and Yerkes were the nearest communities where a general store could be found, but Confluence was proud to have had a post office since 1890. In the 1930s, Roy Sizemore opened a small country store with the Post Office and provided another option for getting supplies. There weren't a lot of people along the river, most of them relatives, but Frances loved those hills and the beauty of the river.

Frances was the daughter of Rubin Colwell and Callie Fields, both born in 1898 and married in 1916. Callie was the child of Jack and Sally Fields. Sally's parents were Sara and Jimmy Huff, both Cherokees, whose forebearers had fled the North Carolina Cherokee Nation in the late 1830s to escape Andrew Jackson and the mass forced migration under the 1830 Indian Removal Act, an attempted genocide known as the Trail of Tears. Sara and Jimmy were not alone in the scattering of Indians and as a result, much Cherokee and Shawnee blood flows in the veins of eastern Kentuckians. On March 3, 1832, the U.S. Supreme Court ruled 5 to 1 that the Georgia Laws pertaining to the Cherokee Nation were unconstitutional and void. President Andrew Jackson, however, ignored the court's decision. The result was the taking of over 25 million acres of Indian lands and the forced relocation of Native Americans to the Oklahoma Territory.

Rubin was born to Sam Colwell and Martha Campbell Colwell, children of Scottish and Irish immigrants who had come to America looking for a better life. In the hollows of Leslie County, there was little opportunity to meet non-relatives for possible marriage. They would often joke, "You know, our family tree don't fork much." But it would have been a serious mistake to be an outsider and make a similar comment. Hill people were proud of their ability to make a living in the wilderness, but also aware that "city folks" thought they were ignorant and backwards. The culture was a closed one by any standard.

As it turned out, Sam Colwell had earlier been married to Sally Fields, but they divorced before any children were born. So, in an oddity of relations, both fathers of Rubin and Callie had been married to Sally at one point. While this was no marrying of relatives, it demonstrates the difficulty hill people had in finding mates outside the family in a sparsely populated region and why so many left after reaching their teens to find both jobs and love. "Martha Colwell was killed by a train when she was 43 years old. She was hit by the cattle guard and thrown up on the hill in pieces. She had to be carried off in a bag.

Sam underwent an operation for an appendectomy under an apple tree without an anesthetic and died due to complications of infection" (Grizzle 2019). Times were not easy for these strong-willed pioneers.

Rubin worked on the railroad and provided a living for his large family. Their first child, Gertrude, was born in 1917 (as a coincidence, on August 19, the same day as Herb Hall). Gertrude was followed by Clarence, Rica, Nita, Frances, Herbert, Anna Lee, Eunice, Bill David, Rosalie, and James. One of the tragedies of the Colwell family was the death of Gertrude at five years of age. She was at her Grandpa Jack's house playing hide and seek when her long dress got too close to the fireplace. Before they could get the fire extinguished, too much damage had been done and she died that night. Rubin and Callie were devastated. Rubin had been considering becoming a preacher until the death of Gertrude. After that, while he remained a devout follower of the Good Book, he "backslid" and wondered how God could let this happen to his sweet child. Callie's strong will held the family together and kept Rubin on the right path (Grizzle 2019). The Kentucky man was the head of the house, but the woman was the matriarch who drove the value system and set the standards for daily life. They raised their remaining ten children with love, devotion, a firm hand, and a Bible.

I am convinced I got my love of the outdoors from my grandfather. I remember as a child, we would make the hour drive across Pine Mountain to Hyden, then down Dry Hill Road for about ten miles to the "Old Home Place" where Rubin and Callie lived. Papaw was an early-to-bed and early-to-rise person, often saying his good night while it was still daylight. In the hills, that was known as "going to bed with the chickens." Then in the pre-dawn, he would rise and prepare for the day ahead, usually with a reading from the Bible. He was born with a severe case of eczema (atopic dermatitis), which he pronounced ex-zee-ma, and it was common for Callie to have to change sheets daily because of bleeding from the sores. But I never heard him complain about his affliction at any time. He embraced life being thankful for the gifts he was given, not troubled by the challenges.

When I awoke, I would go out on the porch with him as he looked across the river at the hillside, stretched his arms high above his head, took a deep breath, bent over, and touched his toes. When he stood back up, he would exhale and say, "Ain't nadur wunnerful!" He innately loved all of God's creations and respected fish, wildlife, and plants as food, but also as his kinsmen. I never knew anyone that loved to see things grow more than Rubin Colwell.

Rubin and Callie Colwell, circa 1975

Callie was the matriarch and had lost the tip of the index finger on her right hand along the way but had no trouble pointing the tipless digit at you and giving you a stern reprimand! Then, as quickly as the scold had come, she would give a devilish look and demand a hug. She was country through and through. She smoked a pipe, rolled her own cigarettes, and occasionally dipped snuff. Not the "smokeless tobacco" we see today, but the fine powder that came in a white container and could either be placed between your lip and gum or sniffed up the nose. She was also one to try and keep up with the gossip.

Down the river, the only phone service was a "party line," which meant several people shared the same service. One would often pick up the phone to make a call and hear a neighbor having a conversation. "I'm on the line" would be heard, and you were supposed to politely hang up and wait until they were finished with their call. When a call came through the line that wasn't meant for you, there would be a single ding instead of a ring. The purpose of this was apparently to alert other users that a call was coming in so they could be respectful and refrain from picking up the phone. But with Mamaw, it was game on! After a short wait to allow the call to be answered, she would very carefully pick up the receiver and listen in on the conversation! She loved getting away with eavesdropping and had a mischievous smile the whole time. I loved both of my grandparents deeply.

Pioneer families were self-sufficient. While Rubin worked for the railroad and brought home a paycheck for things that had to be purchased, the entire family helped grow a garden to supply vegetables that could be preserved through the canning process for the remainder of the year. I have never tasted canned vegetables bought in grocery store that could even begin to compare to the rich flavor contained in home-canned beans, tomatoes, and beets. I remember on my visits to my grandparents during the fall harvest, an organized, yet simple canning operation was set up just off the back porch. The creek that originated with a spring at the top of the mountain flowed by the house and provided clean, cool water for canning and bathing. A well provided drinking water.

A large washtub was used for the canning operation and was placed over a fire built next to the creek, but near enough to the house to limit the distance jars and vegetables had to be carried. Mason or Ball jars were used due to their dependability, and that was no small factor. The family had to survive the winter on the vegetables that were canned. Everyone grew their own chickens for both eggs and poultry. The women and older girls were busy with the canning while the men and boys did the fall butchering. The washtub was filled about three quarters full and the jars with various vegetables were placed in the tub while the water was brought to a boil. This allowed the contents to be sterilized and the rubber gaskets on the lids to expand and seal. As the jars were removed and allowed to cool, an airtight seal resulted. Along with the potatoes and onions that were stored in the cellar, the tomatoes, corn, green beans, beets, cabbage, and cucumbers would provide needed staples for the family. There was an abundance of apples, peaches, and wild berries to make jellies, jams, and apple butter. Cow's milk was turned into butter in a hand-operated churn that separated the fat to make butter. Bartering was a normal means of trade to acquire some necessities such as cornmeal and flour.

In addition to the vegetables, cows, goats, and pigs were kept for milk and meat to go along with the fish and game that were plentiful in Appalachia. Meat was smoked or salt cured. Older boys worked the fields and the girls helped with their younger siblings. Everyone did their part. My first attempt at hunting was when I was around ten years old and asked Papaw if I could take his single shot .410 shotgun squirrel hunting. He said yes, gave me three shells, and sent me on my way. I was taught early how to handle a gun safely, so my parents were not concerned about me going hunting alone.

I made far too much noise to sneak up on a squirrel but did manage to knock a few out of the trees. I took them home as proud as if I had dropped a 12-point buck. In what many would call a wilderness, these innovative pioneers learned to hunt, fish, grow, or make whatever they needed to survive and flourish. To them, the Creator had given all they needed, and they were grateful. If one simply looks and is willing to put in the effort, nature has given us all we need to survive. Sometimes, however, we allow ourselves to be confused by what we *want* and become blind to the cornucopia of what we have been given.

The people of eastern Kentucky were well known for their making of fine moonshine whiskey. Moonshine is the distillate of corn mash and other grains (each man had his own recipe) that came out the drip spout as clear as water and as potent as dynamite! When one drinks fine bourbon today, one is drinking moonshine that has been aged in fire-charred oak barrels to give it the distinct brown color and taste. Moonshiners simply didn't waste time aging it. While Rubin seldom engaged in drinking (in the Baptist religion it is considered the "devil's water"), he got drunk at least once a year, usually around Christmas or New Year's (Grizzle 2019). Frances said he would get so sick he would "vomic [sic] a river." The rest of the year, his children never saw him drink alcohol. Frances had never allowed alcohol to "cross her lips" and would spend the rest of her life without ever having knowingly taken a drink. Moonshine was seen as the devil's water because of the way it caused an otherwise good man to come home and physically abuse his wife and children. Rubin was never known to lay a hand on Callie, but there were a lot of hill men that believed they had the right to "control" their wives. Alcohol was the drug of choice and caused a great deal of pain through its abuse.

Religion was a dominating factor in the lives of hill folk. The Bible gave instruction on how to be a good Christian and treat people in daily life. Much as the Jewish people and other non-Christian religions used books of the Old Testament as rules for food, marriage, business, and other aspects of community living, the New Testament taught Christians how to live a clean and righteous life. Not that it always worked, but they tried. Children were expected to go with their parents to church on Sunday and read the Bible during the week. For most, the Bible was the only book in the home, so it also served to help keep up on reading proficiency.

At the country church, it was unusual to have more than one hymn book with the words to the songs, and many in the congregation couldn't read. The Song Leader would quickly read the line of a song and the group would then sing it. An example would be the Song Leader saying very quickly, "Amazing Grace, how sweet the sound," and the congregation would then sing that line. Followed by the quick line, "That saved a wretch like me," to be sung by the group. Thus, the Song Leader became an important part of the service. Music was, and still is in many religions, an equal form of ministry to preaching. In the Southern Baptist tradition, hill preachers believed they were "called" to preach and nearly all had regular jobs during the week. It wasn't considered a profession then, but rather a profession of faith. Very little of the tithing gift was paid to the preacher, but instead was used to help those in need in the community. Over the years, in all religions, that changed.

The Colwell girls loved gospel music and loved to sing. Rica, Eunice, Frances, and Anna Lee were a quartet throughout their lives. Frances sang alto. In their individual churches after they were married, each was known for her eagerness to be in the choir. Frances made sure to be there every Sunday for Sunday School and church, and on Wednesday night for prayer meetings. Her love of gospel music was her passion, and she sang at tent revivals as well as church whenever she could. Tent revivals were done by travelling preachers who usually worked with local churches to hold services in an open field under a tent every night of the week to "revive" dedication to Jesus. Many evangelists, such as Billy Graham and Oral Roberts, had their start in this way. In Appalachia in the 1930s, families had radio but no television or other forms of entertainment. Family evenings often involved game playing as well as singing and playing of "spoons," mouth harps, and stringed instruments. Religious and bluegrass music were part of the strong fabric of mountain families.

At the end of every service in the Baptist religion, there is an "alter call." The same preacher who, just moments before, had been shouting so loud about hell fire and damnation that his spit was flying everywhere, with a handkerchief to wipe away the sweat, would suddenly be softly delivering an invitation to come forward and give your life to Christ. While he was speaking and giving the invitation, music played either "Come Home" or "Just As I Am," two of the most popular songs for reminding sinners that God is waiting with open arms to receive them. There is something powerful about a small country church filled with people who truly seek salvation, not simply the appearance of faith.

Life along the river was uncomplicated with not a lot to do for children. In summer, they got their work done and wandered the hills hunting for squirrels and rabbits, or looking for mushrooms, nuts, and berries that grew wild in Appalachia. Sometimes they played along the river with a cane pole catching bream, bass, catfish, or drum. It was the best education a child could get. The freedom to explore and learn about nature was a critical part of preparation for adulthood. This basic connection with our natural world was simply accepted as a way of life. Unfortunately, decades later, the youth of America would become prisoners of the electronic age, video games, and cell phones. Connecting our children with nature would become one of the challenges of the 21st century.

With all the chores and studying to do during the school year, there wasn't much time for play. At the end of summer, Callie would take the children to Yerkes or Roy Sizemore's General Store at Confluence. Each child got one new pair of shoes for wearing to school, and they had to last through the winter. Keeping shoes on ten children wasn't cheap and replacing them in a single year was a true burden on the family budget. In the summer, barefoot was the norm. Store-bought candy was a big treat and was usually rock candy, horehound, or licorice. Pop was expensive and hard to come by down the river, so they had to share one bottle among several of them.

Next to Sizemore's store was a swinging bridge that hung across the river and led to one of the family cemeteries. A swinging bridge was built for people to cross rivers by foot and was suspended by ropes from each bank with lashed down boards to walk on. Swinging bridges were common across eastern Kentucky until the state highway department started building vehicle bridges, which made it much more convenient to take a horse and wagon or an automobile to get supplies. I remember the funeral of my "hunchback" cousin, and how the men carried her coffin across the swinging bridge to the cemetery for burial.

While few in Frances' family graduated from High School, education was still extremely important to Rubin and Callie. Uneducated people were easily taken advantage of, and an X for a signature signaled to unscrupulous people, like many that wanted to buy the coal or timber rights, that the signatory was unable to read what they were signing. Many land grabs and con deals were successfully carried out because of the inability of the owner to read and write. The Colwell children were expected to study hard and learn reading, writing, and arithmetic so they would know how to deal in life and not be cheated. Graduating from High School was far less important than these survival skills. Anna Lee talked about the importance of studying:

"There was a spelling bee every year in Hyden, and the winners in each age group would get a *silver dollar*. That was a lot of money then! Frances helped me study for those words the night before. You had to turn down the others in order to keep on going. Herbert turned them all down and got a silver dollar. I got a half dollar because I missed a word." (Grizzle 2019)

Ina Frances Colwell was born on March 1, 1927, the fifth of Rubin and Callie's children. At the age of 13 she had just returned from Lexington, where she received an operation on her leg for polio. A thick cast encased her right leg up to her thigh. She had first been examined by the only doctor within miles, Dr. Koozer in Hyden, who had referred her to the hospital in Lexington for surgery. There was no known cure for polio, but it was considered treatable if caught in the early stages. Because Rubin worked for the railroad, he was able to secure passage for Frances to Lexington. It was hoped an operation would remove the damaged tissue and arrest the spreading. The Frontier Nurses, established by Mary Breckinridge to travel the Appalachian hillsides on horseback or by mule to bring medical treatment where there was none, checked on Frances from time to time but her primary care giver after returning from Lexington was Rica, now the oldest living sister. Rica took great care to ensure Frances had every chance of surviving. She believed deeply in her God and prayed to him every day for the healing of her loving little sister. By all accounts, Frances was kind-hearted and loving as a child. She was deeply religious and, while only having gone through fifth grade, had taken care to learn how to read, write, and do math. The Bible was her favorite book. She believed in Jesus as her Lord and Savior and wanted all to see his love through the way she lived her life, rather than by telling others how to live theirs.

Trained medical professionals were few and far between. Outside the one doctor and three Frontier Nurses, there were only home remedies. These remedies had been developed over the centuries using what the Creator had provided in the forest, rivers, or fields of harvest. Blood poisoning was deadly. The doctors knew no cure, and when Anna Lee's leg became infected with blood poisoning, the doctor sent her home to die.

"The doctor told Mommy to take me home and that I had about three weeks to live. We don't have a medicine to cure blood poisoning. A woman named Sarah told Mommy to make a hot poultice of Epsom salts, flour, sweet milk, and peach leaves. She said to cook it and put it on the wound as hot as I could stand all night long. It was so hot that steam was coming off, and it hurt so bad the neighbor (who was some distance down the river) heard me crying all night long. But it saved my life." (Grizzle 2019)

Frances had been extremely fortunate to receive professional medical treatment. But while she loved school, she was forced to drop out due to her illness. Her brother Herbert, however, came to her after school to tell her what had gone on every day. She was surrounded by siblings who loved her and knew what she was going through was serious. But the cast was itchy and driving her crazy! So, when Callie was busy elsewhere, Anna Lee would sneak Frances down to the river and pour cold water down inside the cast to give some relief. Luckily, the water didn't go far enough down the cast to reach the calf area, so it was still able to perform its duty. They both knew if they were caught, sick or not, there would be a good whipping! (Grizzle 2019)

When the cast was removed, the examination brought smiles to the faces of Dr. Koozer and the Frontier Nurses at his side. While her right calf would be smaller than her left for the rest of her life, she would have a healthy and strong leg. Frances believed with all her heart that God had spared her for a reason. She gave thanks and vowed to always help others. Her life was a testament to that vow. After recovering well enough to travel to Hyden, she went there to help the Frontier nurses take care of the hill people she held so dear and learned important techniques about how to be a caregiver. She didn't know it at the time, but these were skills that would become very important in her future.

As the years passed, she knew she needed to leave the beautiful hills of her home if she were to make something of herself and start a family. By the time she reached her 18th birthday, she was ready to join her sister Nita and brother Herbert in Cincinnati. Nita, three years her elder, had gone earlier and married Gene New. Herbert, though two years younger than Frances, followed and got an apartment near Nita. In the 1940s, teenagers were considered adults and free to strike out on their own. That meant Frances had a place to stay with family watching over her, and she was ready to learn more about the world. Anna Lee came immediately after her because she told Callie, "If I'm a gonna diaper babies all my life and cook and all that, I'm a gonna diaper a few of my own!" She was thirteen. Brother Herbert was about to get two new roommates.

―――

Herb Hall had arrived in Cincinnati and found enough work to afford an apartment and have the basic necessities. By the time Frances arrived, the cold Cincinnati winter had begun to thaw, and the roads and sidewalks were emerging from hibernation. There is something about springtime that has captured the hearts of generations as it seems to wash away the past and open the window for a new beginning. Frances had been in Cincinnati for only a few weeks when she saw a dark-haired, handsome man in her apartment building. She told me later that she immediately said to herself, "That's the man I'm going to marry." She found a way to be properly introduced to this stranger and learned his name was Herb Hall from Harlan, just an hour from where she was raised. He was immediately taken with her as well. Frances was a beautiful, petite woman with brown eyes, black hair and a sweetness that would melt the heart of any man. It was love at first sight, and ten days later they were married. Perhaps Herb knew he only had about twenty years to have and raise a family. Perhaps Frances heard the story of his trauma and believed God had sent Herb for her to take care of and love. But it only took ten days to realize they had each found their mate. After their marriage, they moved back to Harlan. Frances loved Herb Hall with all her heart and Herb loved his new wife like he had never loved anyone. They were headed to a new life together.

CHAPTER 3:

Life In Harlan County

Herb and Frances moved back to Harlan where Herb got a job as a janitor at D & W Motors, a car dealership not far from their house in Dressen on the outskirts of town. While his health condition was considered "poor," he was determined to work and provide for his family as much as his limited health and education would allow. He walked the mile or so to work until he could afford to buy an Army surplus jeep. Life was rapidly returning to normal in 1945. The war had ended in Europe in early May, the same month they were married, and the surrender of Japan took place on board the USS Missouri on September 2. Frances got a job in a small shoe store and their combined incomes allowed them to live in a modest house. A year after their marriage, on May 16, 1946, Frances gave birth to their first child, Larry Milton Hall, named after his grandfather, Milt. Herb was so proud to have a son that the buttons on his shirt were strained by the swelled chest.

Life was a fast pace across America due to the return of men and women from the military, ready to resume building the lives that had been so horribly disrupted. They had a powerful drive and determination to get a normal life going again. After having seen the most atrocious acts of godless brutality that one human can bestow upon another, from the concentration camps in Europe to the prisoner of war camps under the Japanese, these veterans were obsessed with building a world of peace and respect for each other. They wanted to make sure that there would be no more Fuhrers or Emperors, and what they had seen would never happen again. They embarked on a building and growth era with a vigor the likes of which the world had never seen. They were going to make a difference. And they long ago left behind the follower mentality. They had become leaders and they knew it. They had earned the hard way the title of *The Greatest Generation.*

The Servicemen's Readjustment Act of 1944, also known as the GI Bill of Rights, gave a wide range of benefits to the returning veterans, among which was the ability to have a guaranteed low interest loan for a home without a down payment. Also included were funds to support training and education, not just for veterans, but for orphans of war and children of totally disabled veterans. This would become an important factor for one of Herb's children. While he was not one for handouts, he knew he and his fellow veterans had earned each and every benefit a grateful nation would provide. They had just kicked the asses of two of the most powerful, tyrannical military forces the world had ever seen!

Not only did the can-do attitude of the returning veterans impact daily lives, but people in all professions also began to change the world. Breakthroughs in understanding the human genome occurred when Watson and Crick discovered the double helix and how genes can drive susceptibility to disease and natural immunity, as well as how traits are inherited from our parents through gene transfer. General Dwight D. Eisenhower remembered how difficult it had been to move military equipment across the muddy roads of the United States when he was a Lieutenant in World War I. When approached with a plan for the largest investment in infrastructure the U.S. had ever known, President Eisenhower launched the Interstate Highway System that transformed U.S. commerce and transportation forever. Before the building of Interstate 75, our annual trips to Cincinnati and Hamilton, Ohio to see family took over eight hours of driving. After the Interstate was completed, the same trip took half as long. This was a generation that wanted a better life and wasn't about to settle for less.

On Thursday November 3, 1949, Frances gave birth to their second child, Henry Dale Hall. I was born in the three-room "shotgun" house propped on the side of a hill in Dressen and delivered by Dr. Black. The home was modest by any standards, with an outhouse for a toilet but clean and well kept. Just across the two-lane highway was Jack's Drive In and WHLN, Harlan's radio station. Frances worked hard to make a good home for her family, and Herb worked hard to support them. The wages of a janitor and store clerk weren't much, but they were honestly earned, and work was no stranger to either. Herb's family lived nearby, either in Dressen or Elcomb, and were always there for support. His brother Rob had died from a "heart attack" at 27, but the family didn't talk about the circumstances around his death. Abuse of alcohol was the family's whispered reason.

Herb and Frances had decided on two children and wanted desperately to have a daughter to go with the son Herb prized. That was not to be. I was named after Henry Lee Scott, Vernie's son, and someone my father held in great affection. Henry Lee was a strange character. When he came to visit he hardly ever spoke, and when bedtime came, he always got into bed fully clothed except for his shoes. He slept in my bed, and I slept on a "pallet" of quilts on the floor. When I asked him why he didn't undress for bed, he just shrugged. In 1949, a janitor didn't make a lot of money, but the cost of living wasn't as high as today either. A loaf of bread was 14 cents, a gallon of milk was 84 cents, a pound of butter 73 cents, a gallon of gas was 17 cents, a new home averaged $7,500, and the average income was $3,000. Herb made about $25 a week and Frances made less than that, but they got by.

When Herb and Frances first returned to Harlan, Herb was no less the rounder than when he had left for the Army. A pistol was a permanent part of his clothing, but a part you didn't see until there was already fire in his eyes. He still liked to drink and run around with his brothers and friends, but Frances was a mitigating influence. More than once, she went to the local bootlegger bar (Harlan was a dry county), walked up to a drunk Herb, took him by the elbow, and said it was time to go home. No one dared to tease Herb unless they were willing to face the gun he assuredly would pull. On another occasion, he believed Frances had been short-changed on her pay at the little store where she worked. After a few drinks and the onset of darkness, the story goes that he calmly walked down Main Street and emptied his pistol into the store window. Frances quit her job there.

He never mistreated or belittled my mother for coming to fetch him home. He remembered the time on the battlefield when he promised God that he would live a good life if he were spared. He believed God had sent him Frances to be his loving companion, but he was still tortured by a horrendous temper. When he drank, he knew he was not the man he wanted to be. The Halls moved from the house where I was born to one just under the hill, near the bridge that crossed over to Sunshine. It was in this house that Herb found religion. Momma told me that one of his friends would occasionally come by with a case of beer. He and Daddy would sit on the porch and drink until it was gone. Then he would go to bed and sleep it off. Momma convinced him to go to a tent revival with her, and it was at a revival meeting that Daddy accepted Jesus as his Savior. His life changed. Throughout the rest of my life, I never witnessed him having a drink of alcohol of any kind.

The Sunshine bridge house had a bathroom, was heated by a pot-belly stove, and Momma cooked on a kitchen stove that required a fire to heat the top and oven. Coal was of course the fuel of choice. Because of the poor insulation of the houses, pot-belly stoves were well known for making your front side too hot and the back side too cold in winter. People often turned back and forth around the stove to stay warm on both sides. These stoves had a shaker handle at the bottom that was moved side to side to allow the ashes to drop out into a sheet metal container underneath. Apparently, I liked to eat the ash chunks that had been shaken out of the stove and everyone was on the lookout to keep me from my unapproved snacks.

Just before I started first grade, we moved from Dressen to Fairview, a community across the river from Harlan High School, where Larry would be in fourth grade and I would begin first grade. While called a high school, it would be years before the city could afford to have separate elementary and high schools. Our house at 209 May Street was nicer than the one we had lived in at Dressen but was still small and had only about four small rooms in the living quarters and a bathroom. Out back was an eight-by-eight foot smoke house where Daddy smoked ham, brisket, and other meats for preservation that he had bought from farmers he knew. We didn't have a freezer to preserve food except for the very small area at the top of the Frigidaire.

Times were different then, and children of all ages walked to and from school without adult escort. For my first few days of school, Momma walked with me across the bridge to make sure I knew the way, but then I was expected to walk with the other kids on my own. I apparently didn't care for school that much in first grade and quite a few times Momma had to walk me back after I decided I wanted to go home before school was over. A few spankings later and a better understanding of my responsibilities, everything went fine. I came to love school and learning, a joy I have never outgrown.

One sunny afternoon in the spring of 1956, I walked home as usual, flipped off my penny loafers that were just a tad too big for me on the front porch, and went inside. What I saw was very confusing. Daddy was sitting on the side of the bed in the living part of the house where Larry and I also shared a bed. He had a kitchen chair in front of him, chair facing away, with his head on his arms rested on the high back. Underneath his arms was a pillow, and he seemed to be in great pain.

"Daddy, what's wrong?"

Momma appeared from the kitchen and quickly ushered me out of the room. "Daddy's having real bad chest pains. The doctor is coming, and you need to stay out of the way."

"Is he okay? Momma, I'm scared."

"He'll be fine, honey. The doctor is on his way. I want you to go next door to Mrs. Hagy's and stay there until I come get you."

Mrs. Hagy had a daughter named Susan that was near my age, and we played together regularly. I felt comfortable going there, but still worried about my father. The question was answered soon enough when an ambulance arrived, Daddy was carried out on a stretcher, and I watched as Momma left with them. I was crying and knew something really bad had happened. At six years old, it's difficult to process things we consider "grown up." Children are shielded from harm, both physically and mentally, but children also have a keen sense of their surroundings when fear sets in. Survival is an innate defense system that is extremely complicated. I wondered if I would ever see my father again. Was he going to die? Mrs. Hagy tried in vain to calm my tears and reassure me, but I was a "sensitive child" and often had my emotions on my sleeve. That would not change for many years.

Daddy survived a massive heart attack caused by the constant irritation of the shrapnel against his pericardium (the sac around the heart). His poor condition, as identified at his Army discharge, had culminated in a near death myocardial infarction and severe angina that rendered him totally disabled, as classified by the military, and ended his hopes of doing so many of the things he enjoyed. He loved to hunt, especially coon hunt, and fish. Up until the time of his heart attack, he often went out in his Willys jeep with his buddies to sit around a campfire all night listening to the howling of the hounds as they chased raccoons. I am told he took me on a hunt once and I fell out of the back of the Jeep. I don't recall going with him after that. One knows immediately when the dogs have treed a coon because the barking changes to a totally different cadence and howl. The men quickly run to the treed coon and shoot him out. Good coon dogs were highly prized possessions. Conversely, a coon dog that retreated from a fight with a coon (which could defend itself vigorously) was despised.

Daddy once took us to a "coon on the log" gathering, where people converged on a riverbank with a big place to picnic, and the men would tie a live raccoon to a log and anchor it out in the water. They then turned their coon dogs loose and sent them out to get the coon off the log. A coon is a vicious animal when cornered and being tied to a log in the middle of a river with hounds swimming towards it is about as cornered as it can get. I saw several dogs come back to shore with half their ear gone or large gashes on their nose, just to have their owners beat or shoot them for quitting. Daddy didn't approve of this mistreatment and made sure we knew it. I decided then and there that I would not be a coon hunter if I had to treat animals that way. To me, hunting involves integrity, ethics, and a respect for the animals that are hunted as well as the hunting companions. The cruelty I witnessed fit no part of that definition, and I spent the rest of my life opposing that kind of "hunter." I still do.

After the heart attack, the extent of Daddy's physical activities were truncated to such a narrow description that he was just one step above an invalid. After recovering and receiving official confirmation of being a totally disabled veteran, he was assured of a modest but steady income in the form of a pension for the rest of his life. In addition, he was able to keep his $10,000 government life insurance policy. These were extremely important to him. The circumstances that made him eligible for these benefits were a high price to pay, but it gave him the income security he had previously lacked as a janitor to plan for his family's future.

With the GI Bill and his guaranteed pension, he was able to buy a house in Loyall about three miles downriver from Harlan from his sister, Pearl. Pearl and her husband, Ross, were childless, and Ross had a good job with the railroad. With no children, Pearl became very finnicky about her house and how you behaved there. Truth be known, Pearl didn't like kids and I think the feeling was mutual. Going to her house was not one of our excitement moments. But when she and Ross decided to move a few miles downriver to Dayhoit to a house next to her brother, Elb, and his wife, Ethel, it created the opportunity at the right time for Herb and Frances to acquire their own home.

CHAPTER 4:
Living in Loyall

Daddy's oldest sister, Nannie, and her husband, "Pop," lived across the street and had one grown daughter, Jean, living in Illinois. They also owned Pop's Café, a small diner on Eversole Street in Harlan near the courthouse. Tom "Pop" Bradberry was a tall, kind man from Alabama who always made us kids feel welcome. Pop's Café was next door to Mr. Cummins' shoe repair shop and had about four booths and two tables, one of which sat next to the juke box and was Nannie's "roost," where she had coffee and cigarettes all day while Pop took care of the short orders up front at the grill and a cook in the back did the hot meals. There was a counter with about six stools that were anchored to the floor so kids like me couldn't knock them over while seeing how fast they would spin. Momma eventually became the cook in the kitchen. Everyone who knew Momma was aware of her country cooking prowess. Pop's was filled every morning by people who wanted Frances' gravy and biscuits for breakfast and her chicken and dumplings for dinner.

By the time I was in 6th grade, Momma was getting up at 3:30 a.m. and driving the three miles from Loyall to Pop's Café to make the big pot of gravy, homemade biscuits, bacon, sausage, fried potatoes, and all the fixings for a hearty Kentucky breakfast. After making all that, she came back home by 6:30 to make Larry and me the same gravy and biscuits before we went to school. After making sure we were fed and on our way, she went back to Pop's to cook the dinner meal. I don't recall Daddy ever offering to fix breakfast for us, but then I never saw him cook anything except on a grill. I once said, "Momma, we can get ourselves up and fix a bowl of cereal for breakfast. You don't have to drive back and forth like this to get us up and off to school." Her indignant reply was, "I'll not send my children to school on cold cereal!"

Dinner for hill people is the noontime meal. The evening meal is supper. While Daddy was not able to work, Momma worked hard enough for both. In addition to her job at the café, she also cleaned house for a few people in Loyall and did odd jobs for the church to make extra money. A war pension and Momma's small income didn't bring a lot of money into the house, but with a mortgage of $65 a month and grocery bills of $25 a week from Mack's or the A&P, they were able to take care of us. We never knew we were poor. We just thought there were other people with more money. I remember by the time I was a senior in high school in 1967, Daddy's disability check finally reached $300 a month. The average annual family of four income in 1967 was just under $10,000 and, to many, we were in poverty. But we didn't think so.

Our home had a living room, kitchen, two small bedrooms and a bathroom. The small, enclosed back porch gave a little extra room for storage. There was a full basement with the stoker furnace and hot water heater that required a fire be built in the small stove each time hot water was needed. Beside that was the coal bin. Because stoker coal was fed into the furnace by an auger, each piece was much smaller than the big coal chunks used for a pot belly stove. One of my jobs was to fill the coal hopper each night so there was always a fire in the winter. The rest of the basement was concrete and gave some room for storage and an extra bed for Larry and me if we had visitors. Larry and I shared a small bedroom with twin beds. Our air conditioner in the summer was a box fan in the window or the front porch after the sun went down.

The worst part about getting ready for school each morning was brushing my teeth. We only had the small bathroom that was barely large enough for the tub, toilet, and sink. Daddy had the Louisville Courier

Journal delivered each morning, and he calmly took his place on the toilet, reading the paper while I had to stand less than a foot away and brush my teeth. That's the way it was, and Daddy didn't see the need to postpone his morning ritual until Larry and I were off to school. Everyone in our neighborhood was in the same relative income bracket, but we had all the true needs of food, shelter, medical care and, most important, love. Even today, I believe we were rich with the things that really mattered.

Daddy still worried about bills and remained haunted by memories of being wounded, as well as the ominous prediction of "twenty years to live." All the doctors at the VA hospital in Johnson City, Tennessee were amazed that he was still alive and commented on that to him at each visit! As a result of this unbelievable lapse in sensitivity to the patient, we watched him constantly worry that each breath would be his last. He refused to even take short walks around the neighborhood as prescribed by our family physician, Dr. Foley, because he was paranoid he would have another heart attack and die before he was able to "see Larry have his eighteenth birthday" (Lee 2019). He often had nightmares and would wake us all with his loud moaning. To anyone who thinks PTSD is not real and a scar for life, I beg to differ. When I witnessed the times he could have enjoyed doing what he loved to do, like the relatively easy pastime of fishing, but denied himself the simple pleasures out of fear of dying, I was heartbroken. I vowed that I would never live life afraid of dying, but instead live each day as if it were my last. None of us is promised this evening, much less tomorrow. Throughout my life, I have tried to live with that fact and treat each sunrise as a gift from my Creator. Even today, when I hunt with friends in a duck blind, as the horizon begins to glow, I always look to the sky and give thanks for another day, then turn to my hunting partners and say, "Thank you for sharing your sunrise with me." How we use that sunrise is up to us.

My Appalachian Trail

We moved to Loyall for the beginning of my 2nd grade. It was a longer walk to school, but not by much. Loyall had a population of only a few hundred while Harlan boasted 3,200 as the County Seat. Our house was at 117 Cedar Street, but mail wasn't delivered in Loyall, so we had Box 384 at the Loyall Post Office and Harbor's Barber Shop. The headwater reach of the Cumberland River was just across the street from our house and where I spent many summer hours when I wasn't riding my bike, playing kick the can, or "thumbing" to Harlan to go to the swimming pool or play little league baseball. The thumbing (hitchhiking) corner was between the corner gas station and Mike's Drive In, and no one gave a second thought about an 11-year-old thumbing a ride to Harlan. People knew where we were going by our little league uniform or swimsuits rolled up in a towel and would often take us all the way to the baseball field and let us off there. It was a different time, and the thought of molesting or harming a child in any way was unthinkable. This was Harlan County. The law was called to cut you down from the tree and carry your dead body away, not to arrest you if you hurt a child. Everyone knew us. Everyone took care of us.

Throughout Harlan County, various creeks gradually merged to create the mainstem of this beautiful river. At low water stage, I could easily walk across the river at the riffles looking for bait. Each time I cross that mighty Cumberland River in central Tennessee, I am amazed at the nearly one-mile bridge that spans it. The rocks I turned over were sandstone or shale, and many times I waited patiently for the water to clear to see if our prey was there, unaware it was about to become bait. To catch a crawdad by hand, we put one hand behind it and slowly "sneaked up on it." There was something, even then, about the connectivity with nature that swirled in our DNA and made us feel alive when interacting with highly adapted creations. Another popular bait was a "grampus," the larva of a Dobson fly. They were black and had fierce pincers. But the bass loved them!

On Cedar Street were families that all worked hard and cared for each other. L.C. and Louise Hatfield had two children, Diane and Hal, and liked to go to Norris Lake just over the border in Tennessee. They often invited me to go with them and taught me how to water ski. I loved them dearly, and they treated me like family. Up the street were Julia Mae Allen, and not far from her were Larry and Johnny Farmer. Julia was also like a sister. I was the only boy besides her kin that Mrs. Allen would let visit with Julia in her bedroom. Larry and Johnny Farmer were good friends all through school. Next door to us were the McGlothins, with six boys and one girl, Diane. Mrs. McGlothin often referred to Larry as "son number seven" and me as "son number eight." Diane became like a sister to me, as did the other girls on the street. I ran the river with Diane's brother, Jerry, who mentored me about fishing and using a car top boat. A car top boat was just that, the top of an old coupe car that had been cut off at the junk yard and flipped over to use as a boat. We could get one if we all chipped in our lawn mowing or pop bottle return money for about $5, its value as scrap metal.

A car top boat was perfect for two and could handle three if they were skinny like me. The struts that connected the top to the car body were perfect to lean your fishing rod or cane pole against and wait for a bite. Daddy let me use his Nelson Pistol Grip with a Bristol 38, five-foot metal rod and an old Ambassador reel. You couldn't cast it, so we pulled out all the line we needed by making loops in one hand, spun the hook, sinker, and bait with our other hand and threw it out as far as we could. A scrap board worked just fine as a paddle. Some might say we were 20th Century Huckleberry Finn's, but we didn't think so. We were simple country kids who lived *with* the other species of nature and were taught to respect them.

Our lives were solidly utilitarian, and the fish and wildlife we were able to secure were part of our subsistence culture. Over the years, the river began to change in water quality because of the coal silt and increased mud from mine erosion, as well as the sewage outfall. We didn't have a sewage treatment plant in Loyall, so the sewer pipes just emptied straight into the river. We found the fishing below the outfall was better for catfish but were careful not to tell Momma where we caught them when we took them home for supper. One of my chores was to carry the paper sacks from the grocery store we used as garbage bags and toss them off the bridge as I walked to school. There was no garbage dump. No garbage collection. No alternative. We all did what we had to do. It is ironic that I spent my entire professional career working to clean up America's rivers.

Living behind me was one of my best friends, Larry Mize. Larry was only a year older than me but twice my size. But so were a lot of people. I was small for my age and never broke 100 pounds until I was in 9th grade. Larry had severe asthma and couldn't do a lot of the games that required running, but we still spent a lot of time fishing. Karen Lowry lived three houses down on our side of the street and Jimmy Stanfill lived across the street from Karen. Most of the kids in our neighborhood, all the way up to the swinging bridge that took you over to Lawnvale, were near the same age. We had a lot of fun playing all year round. I still consider those wonderful friends as part of my family.

The Cumberland River and adjacent hills marked one side of our neighborhood, and the train yard and railroad tracks on the other side of the hollow marked the other. We could sit on our front porch and see the cars coming and going at Mike's Drive In across the river by the thumbing corner, while each night I went to sleep hearing Louisville & Nashville (L&N) trains bang against each other at the train yard behind us as the cars "coupled." Soon the warning bells began as another loaded train moved out of the yard and over the crossing that led to Blackbottom. I am still comforted by the sound of train whistles in the night. It brings a certain peace and innate feeling of safety. I never knew how Blackbottom got its name, but assumed it was because of all the coal dust spilled along the tracks as the cars headed out to supply the nation with energy. The ground between Highway 413 behind us and the railroad tracks was owned by L&N and was always vacant. That meant we had a place to play baseball in the summer and football in the winter. The railroad people didn't mind as long as we stayed clear of the trains, and we were happy to oblige. We had been taught well about the dangers. Accidents happened, even to adults. Frankie Crider's father was killed while trying to help couple some cars together. We all knew the warnings were valid. The train folks would often send out one of their brush hogs to mow the weeds so we could play.

During summer when we weren't playing baseball, going swimming in Harlan, or spending hours on the river, there were the mountains to roam. Harlan County hills are beautiful by any standard and bring with them the melding traditions of Indians, Irish, and Scottish who settled in the wilderness and carved out a living. This was home. Hours were spent discovering where a creek originated from the springs with water that had never needed nor been touched by chlorine. The limestone caves and underground rivers create a world beneath the surface that few have ever seen. I was always one to shun tight quarters, so I left the cave exploration to others. But the cool air at their entrance was a blessing in the sweltering summer heat.

When fall began to arrive, the beauty of the deciduous forest leaves once again provided proof that the Creator loves art. With all the good things the river gave us, there was also the unforgiving side. When the hills are so close together that there are few flat places to store water during heavy rains, flash flooding becomes a real issue. During the late winter and spring of each year, everyone watched the weather to see if we were in danger of having to evacuate. Flash floods are difficult to describe to someone that has never witnessed the rapid accumulation of drainage from the small tributaries into the mainstem, creating a literal wall of water that moves down the valley. Our house was on the high side of the riverbank, but the houses across the street were threatened each time flash floods occurred.

The closest our house ever came to having the living quarters flooded was when the water reached the top step of the basement stairs. The

Harlan County Rescue Squad came around in the middle of the night, banging on doors and telling people to get out as fast as we could. When we returned after the river subsided, we opened the basement door and took one step down into water. The basement was completely full and the furnace under water, but the living part of the house was still dry. It wasn't until after I was married and in graduate school at LSU that water made it up into the house. When my new wife, Sarah, and I went to help Momma clean up, the water mark was four feet up the wall. I told her she had no reason to remain in this dangerous area and should move out. She did, and many years later a Corps of Engineers flood control project rerouted the river around Harlan and left the historic channel that had provided me with so many peaceful memories a dead pool. But at least some level of flood protection had been provided.

My walk to school was down Cedar Street to the Loyall bridge by the First Baptist Church. Momma was a regular there, sang in the choir and helped clean. Across the bridge was John and Goldie's Corner Store on one side and Claude White's General Store on the other. The Loyall Theater, where I had my first job tending the popcorn machine, was also on that corner. Down to the right a couple of blocks was Loyall High School. Our Chief of Police, and only policeman, was Cody Long. Cody was an ex-con that Loyall had hired when it was *the* place to come play the slots and drink bootleg whiskey. We were told that Cody had killed a man in a fight and spent time in prison. For Cody Long, fear was something you could find in the dictionary.

But he loved this little town and proceeded to clean it up. By the time we moved there, all the slot machines had been confiscated and were stored in the attic above the firehouse, bootleggers had been shut down, and peace restored. Cody's spot to sit was in front of Claude White's store at our only stop light on an old milk crate so he could watch the traffic. That also let the traffic know Cody was watching them. He loved us kids and wasn't shy about grabbing us by the collar and telling us to behave ourselves. We listened and obeyed. My bicycle was stolen once, and Cody showed up about two days later with the bike. A boy from near Baxter, a couple of miles up the road, had stolen it, and Cody wasn't about to let that happen. Cody Long was law.

Loyall was called a High School, but all twelve grades attended. The teachers there were more than teachers. They were role models and second parents. Our teachers in grade school, Mrs. Meadors in third grade and Mrs. Unthank in fourth grade, were like second mothers to us. We behaved in class because punishment at home was much worse than what we would get at school. I was spanked with a wooden paddle by Mr. Smith in 7th grade and by the principal in high school. I deserved it and didn't dare complain to my parents. Once they found out why a teacher had punished me, I ran the risk that Daddy would have had me "cut a switch" from the local bush for *him* to use in punishing me. I learned early not to bring one back that was too small to make the punishment hurt less. If I did, he would cut one, and it would *not* be small.

He never hit me with a switch or belt anywhere but on my rear end, but he made his point. For those who think this type of punishment is child abuse, I suggest you look closely around you at the growing trend in society of disrespect for elders and each other. I strongly believe this comes from not learning that everything we do in life has a reward. Some are good rewards, some are not. One truth spans generations: what parents do not correct in the home, society will inherit and be forced to correct in a less desirable manner and at much greater cost. I treasure those times because there was never an angry face swatting me, but one of love and expectation that I become a better person.

Loyall, like all schools in Harlan County, had the basic equipment but nothing more. There was a gym for PE and basketball. Outside the main building was the playground between the cafeteria and the house trailers that were used as classrooms. When I was in third grade, a new building was constructed to replace some of the trailers, but at least four were used as classrooms throughout my time there. We only had two sports: football and basketball. No track. No baseball. No wrestling. Most of us weren't aware that in more affluent parts of the state, there were actually high school baseball and track teams! Our high school football games were played at the field in Harlan because Loyall didn't have a field. But our teachers went above and beyond to make sure there were school clubs to help us prepare for life in a community.

They taught home economics, mainly for girls, that prepared them to manage a household budget and live as adults. We also had to take Civics, where we began class with the pledge of allegiance, learned how our government works, and how to participate as citizens. We were taught to respect our flag and country. I wish schools today taught both home economics and civics to prepare young men and women to be productive members of society. In our haste to increase scholastic knowledge, I fear we may have abandoned essential education.

In May 1961 in Mr. Phillip Smith's 7th grade class, we listened intently to the radio as the broadcast of Alan Shepard's historic flight made him the first American in space, signaling the "space race" with the Soviet Union. One month earlier, on April 12, the Soviet Cosmonaut Yuri Gagarin became the first human in space and a fever pitch of excitement engulfed the world at the prospect of space travel. Shepard's fifteen-minute flight, dubbed "Freedom 7," was watched by an estimated 45 million viewers. Shortly after Shepard's flight, President John F. Kennedy announced his intent to put a man on the moon "by the end of this decade" and the Gemini and Apollo missions were born under the recently created National Aeronautics and Space Administration (NASA). Mr. Smith took advantage of this teaching opportunity to quiz us on what we had just heard. "What does the term 'AOK' mean?" "How much time did Shepard spend in space?" "What is the difference between an astronaut and a cosmonaut?" Teachers at Loyall did not have a plethora of teaching aids and, therefore, were keen on using every event, every opportunity possible, to have us think outside our little mountain community.

One day, the door opened in Mr. Smith's class and Mrs. Claire Hill walked into the room. She was an English teacher and asked if there were any who would like to be in the Speech Club. She said there would be travel to speech festivals in Barbourville and possibly even Lexington. My arm shot up like a rocket! Anything that would get me out of class occasionally was welcomed, and the possibility of going to those exotic places was more than I could handle! After I joined, I asked, "What is Speech Club?"

I had no idea that would be one of the life changing days for me. Throughout my career, the ability to communicate has been paramount to success. I learned the importance of standing in front of a group, knees shaking and heart racing, while calmly reciting a poem or reading prose in a way that conveyed the inner feelings of the author. Most important, I learned that communication is the *conveyance* of a thought or idea, not just the delivery. The object of the communication must stop long enough to listen to the thought being delivered and understand it. I went on to compete in festivals throughout high school and continued to improve my "hillbilly" way of saying things so people would understand that the way we talked didn't mean we were ignorant. In fact, the hillbilly language is steeped in old English, and the similarity is evident when one reads Chaucer or Milton. It is a noble language that has survived the centuries where others have faded into obscurity. Those who confuse dialect with ignorance make a serious error in judgement. Learning to speak clearly and distinctly is one of the greatest leadership skills one can have. A leader will have no followers if her or his vision is not understood.

Mr. Smith also took advantage of my involvement in speech to have me learn the poem "Richard Cory." He knew many of us came from very poor homes but wanted to instill the message that happiness isn't tied to money, but rather from peace within.

> "Whenever Richard Cory went down town,
> We people on the pavement looked at him;
> He was a gentleman from sole to crown,
> Clean favored, and imperially slim.

And he always quietly arrayed,
And he was always human when he talked;
But still he fluttered pulses when he said,
'Good Morning,' and he glittered when he walked.
And he was rich—yes, richer than a king,
And admirably schooled in every grace;
In fine, we thought that he was everything,
To make us wish that we were in his place.
So on we worked, and waited for the light,
And went without the meat, and cursed the bread;
And Richard Cory, one calm summer night,
Went home and put a bullet through his head."

– *Edward Arlington Robinson*

I accept my bias, but I believe there was a magic in the halls of country schools that attracted the best teachers. Wonderful teachers like Mrs. Hill, who taught me to not be afraid to speak in public; Mrs. McFarland, who demanded we understand that hard work accompanied anything worth having; Mr. Smith, who made us realize how rich we were in the important things and happiness cannot be gauged by appearances; and Mrs. Grant for her constant love and affection for us all. From this I learned that education is tied neither to buildings nor supplies, but to people who are dedicated to their students and love teaching.

The years I spent at Loyall were also significant times for America. While there were relatively few black people in Harlan County, I grew up seeing different treatment for the ones that were there. Water fountains with signs that read "whites only" or "coloreds only" were common, as required by the separate but equal doctrine of Jim Crow law. I had little interaction with black people until my 12th grade, after the all-white Harlan and all-black Rosenwald High Schools were consolidated in 1964 under federal court orders that abolished Jim Crow. Separate but equal was declared no longer acceptable under United States law. All of this went with little notice at Loyall because there were no black people in the school district. I don't recall being overtly taught to think of black people as less than white people, but the behavior of white people and the way they talked sent the message.

My mother, one who didn't have a hurtful bone in her body, said of a black woman singing on television, "She's beautiful for a colored woman." I thought that was an odd thing to say. Is beauty different because of skin color? I came to realize over the years that prejudice and discrimination are tied to power and the need to feel superior. Economics is a clear driver in the phenomenon and often dictates the degree of prejudice. If one is professionally and financially secure and can view themselves as successful, then the need to denigrate someone else because of their skin seems to diminish. Conversely, insecurity and the lack of self-esteem gives rise to prejudice as a means of self-elevation.

I believe it was meant for me to attend Harlan High my last year to expose me to a race for which I had little interaction. It helped me learn that color is a pigmentation, not a character trait, and served me well throughout my life. By getting to know my new black friends, I saw that they were worried about their future and what they would do after graduation. Would their boyfriend or girlfriend break up with them? It was a blessing to get to know kids like Maurice Hollingsworth, Willie Menter, George Ann Martin, Allen Pope, and Edgar Watts and to clearly see they were no different than me. There are certainly black people who demonstrate poor behavior. But I have seen no shortage of white people who display the same, or worse. There is no correlation between the color of one's skin and the character of the individual. But how one behaves towards other races says a great deal about *their* character.

Martin Luther King, Jr. led the civil rights movement of the 1960s and followed the blueprint of peaceful civil disobedience used by Mahatma Gandhi in India to shame the British into allowing home rule. King knew that just over 10% of the U.S. population could not force change, neither through the vote nor violence. Rather, drawing out the cruelty of oppressive bigotry through non-violent actions forced the good among the majority to demand that their brethren be treated with dignity and respect. The shameful violence of the police in Alabama and across the southern United States was shown on national television and forced all those who had chosen the easy path of ignoring the problem to see the inhumanity that was being imparted.

Peaceful protesters were beaten with clubs, bitten by police dogs, and assaulted with fire hoses before being arrested. In other cases, young people who came south to help in the peaceful protests were pulled over on country roads, beaten, murdered, and buried in shallow graves simply because they believed we were all created equal. This was more than the good white people of America could ignore. In 1963, President John F. Kennedy proposed the Civil Rights Act to legally defend the rights of *all* Americans and end the era of Jim Crow. After his assassination, President Lyndon Johnson carried the battle to Congress and, on July 2nd after a drawn-out battle with the Senate, signed the Civil Rights Act of 1964. The following year on August 6, 1965, Public Law 89-110, the Voting Rights Act, was passed to remove the final legal obstacle to true equality. Black Americans had stood their ground in peaceful civil disobedience, and white Americans had heard their pleas for justice and demanded that their Congressional representatives rectify a wrong. It was a good day for America.

Another significant set of events was manifested in the early 1960s by a Louisville boxer by the name of Cassius Marcellus Clay, Jr. Clay was a heavy bragger and constantly taunted his opponents. His nickname of the "Louisville Lip" was one he prized, but the title he gave himself was the one that stuck over time: "The Greatest." The 1960s were a highly turbulent time in America due to the Civil Rights movement and constant Vietnam war protests. The country was divided based on differing beliefs of the meaning of duty and fairness. Riots were common and tensions were at a fever pitch. But Clay, who would later accept Islam and change his name to Muhammad Ali, brought civil rights and the Vietnam war together on one stage.

Aunt Rika's son, Danny Browning, was one of the most religious people I had ever met, and I still feel that way. He didn't just talk about his beliefs, he staunchly lived by them. When he was drafted into the Army and claimed "Conscientious Objector" status because he refused to try and kill his fellow man, I didn't know what that meant. Momma explained it to me in a way I understood by saying Danny could not kill another human, nor assist in anyone else killing, because he believed the Ten Commandments were real and we were expected to live by them. Had it not been for Danny and my absolute belief he was telling the truth, I would not have understood when Muhammad Ali did the same. But with Ali, he put *everything* he had earned on the table to be taken away by refusing to follow the law and go into the Army. I couldn't believe someone would go to jail, allow all their world boxing titles to be stripped, and start all over because of religious beliefs, but he did. Whether I respected him up until that time, I can't recall. But I respected him then.

I knew he wasn't a coward. He exchanged punches with Sonny Liston, who had knocked a grown cow to its knees with one punch, and broke Liston's collar bone in the 7th round with a straight jab. No, he truly believed in his God and put all else second to that belief. In my mind, he had become "The Greatest." Many of us talk about our beliefs but shirk away when our livelihood or possessions are threatened. Not Muhammad Ali. I honored and respected him until the day he died. I am irritated today by some self-declared martyrs who don't really believe they will lose anything by taking a stance for peace or equality but want to be placed in the same category as Ali. At a time when scores of young Americans were going to Canada to avoid the draft, Ali stayed and defended his beliefs within the U.S. system of Justice. Athletes and other "heroes" of today are not faced with prison and/or the removal of titles. Ali *knowingly* gave up everything for *his* beliefs.

Another historical, though not proud, moment occurred when I was in ninth grade. One of my good friends was Jim Boggs. Jim lived on the other side of Loyall near Rio Vista, up on the side of a hill. His mother was a wonderful woman and teacher, and I loved her very much. We were in French class with Mrs. Boggs when her youngest son Parker burst into our classroom trailer and blurted out, "They shot the President!" Mrs. Boggs went pale, then ran out to get more information. When she returned, she had concern in her eyes and told us that President John F. Kennedy had been shot and killed. We didn't fully understand the impact killing a President would have but knew through our classes in Civics that was not the way we settle political disputes in America. It was a terrible day. To prepare us for the actions that would occur in our government, Mrs. Boggs reminded us that Vice President Lyndon Johnson would step up to be our President, and that our founding fathers had anticipated as many circumstances as possible in the drafting of our constitution. We had no idea that nearly five years later his brother would also be assassinated while campaigning for the same office.

CHAPTER 5:
The Exodus

In our home, Larry and my father had a very special relationship. Larry was the rebel type with bright blue eyes, Brylcreem-covered black hair, and a wild streak to go with it. He had no love for school and would have been happy to leave at any time. Partly due to a slight stutter when he talked and some teasing from other kids, he got into more fights than I ever did and was always on the defensive. Because of age difference and views on life, Larry and I never reached the point of being close as siblings, even later in life. But Larry was one of the few my father would talk to, and he would give Larry anything within his power.

I was at first jealous of a closeness between them that I couldn't seem to achieve, but eventually accepted that it was I who was the odd one. I loved school and wanted to be more than a coal miner or work on the railroad. I never felt above these honest jobs, but I wanted to use my mind and enjoyed learning immensely. This didn't fit the custom in our family of working with our hands. Daddy seemed to easily become frustrated with me when I would say I intended to go to college and have a "desk job," and I don't recall having an exchange of ideas with him more than two or three times in my life. He loved sports but only attended one game when I played little league baseball and only one of my high school football games. That's just the way it was. My strong relationship with my mother, however, made up for any distance my father showed me.

Momma was always there, working hard at the café and then coming home to cook me breakfast before school, cleaning houses to help make ends meet, and keeping our home so clean it squeaked. One thing I could not handle was seeing my mother on her hands and knees scrubbing our floors. I immediately stopped and got down to help her, pleading with her to put something soft under her knees. I knew about her childhood polio and was always concerned she had more pain than she conceded. I volunteered to help her often, but I now know not enough. There could never be enough for the woman that held our family together. I had her brown eyes, the Colwell features, and was often closer to my Colwell cousins than those on my Hall side. I think that added to the distance my father kept between us. But Momma was always the peacemaker and stood by Daddy in every way. No woman could have been a better wife and mother.

Before going into the Army, Larry had convinced Daddy to trade in the family car and buy a new 1965 Ford Mustang, 289 cubic inches with four in the floor, and *the* car to have for a young man. Momma was devastated. When Larry and Daddy drove the car home and parked it out front, Momma came to the door and saw the new car for the first time.

"What in the world is that? I ain't had a new dress in a year, and you come home with that for a family car!"

"If you ain't had a new dress, it's your own fault!" my father snapped.

He clearly tried to relive as much of his younger days as he could through Larry. Deep down, he still loved the hell raiser. Momma was also upset because this was the third car my father had bought because Larry had wanted it, with a 1958 Ford he bought for Larry still sitting in the back yard broken down. Only having one car for the family created challenges when there was the need to get to Pop's for work and buy groceries, while having the understanding that the car was there mainly for my brother. In addition, Larry spent little time at home. He was in love and nearly lived at the house of his girlfriend in Baxter, with the car simply sitting outside her home all day. However, when Larry went into the Army for two years and I was able to get my license, I became the beneficiary of the Mustang!

With Larry not there, Daddy had no issue with me driving it, and I took advantage of that whenever he would let me. But when Larry got out of the Army, that changed.

I was a senior in high school in 1967, and Larry had come back home full of piss and vinegar. Both my father and mother could not have been happier. Larry and I had never had a strong relationship, but I loved my brother and was grateful he had survived Vietnam. At the end of my junior year of high school, Loyall was reduced to an elementary school, and the county high schools of Loyall, Hall, and Wallins were consolidated into the new James A. Cawood High School. Rather than ride the bus the extra miles to Cawood, and a small-minded football coach who thought school should be secondary to football, I decided to transfer to Harlan High School for my senior year. I met wonderful friends for life there, among them Jimmy Seals, Homer Fortney, Jerry Blanton, Doran Harris, Roger Noe (an old friend from Fairview), Mike Forester, Karen Shumate, Robert Yost, Judy Smithers (who would marry Larry and become my sister-in-law), and numerous others to whom I remain grateful today. I was joined by my Loyall friends Diane McGlothin, George Ella Hoskins, Susan Noe (who had gone to Harlan all through school), and Rita Harbor. Together with our new classmates, we made wonderful life memories.

On this day, I got my ride home from school as usual and my father let me take the Mustang back to school for an event that was happening at five o'clock. Most of the time I would have thumbed home when the car was needed, but he let me take it because the event was supposed to be over at six. I was told to be home by six thirty so Larry could take it out for the evening. Things went a little long at school and I was also visiting with my friends, so I didn't get home until seven, a half hour late. That's when my father essentially ended our relationship for life, whether or not that was his intent.

I walked in the door of our small house and put the keys on the cabinet housing the TV where they usually stayed. Before I could look around, my father was literally one inch from my face with his eyes glaring: "Where the hell have you been?"

I had never heard my father say anything stronger than shit, so I knew he was really upset, and I honestly didn't understand why. Because of his condition, I lived my life keeping my personal problems from him that might upset him out of fear it would trigger the fatal heart attack we all knew would eventually come. I was stunned and afraid he might have that heart attack then and there! I knew I was late, but to a teenager, 30 minutes isn't very late. I wasn't sure what to do next.

"Larry waited here for fifteen minutes and then said he wasn't waitin' any longer, and he would just get a ride with somebody else while you are out galivantin' around," Daddy barked. His eyes were wild with a rage I had seldom seen.

"The thing went a little longer than I thought, and I didn't think you'd want me to leave early," I said.

He immediately barked, "You don't care about anybody but yourself! You never have and never will!" He raised his hand and I thought he was going to hit me. By this time, my eyes were welling with tears. Nothing he could have done could have hurt me more than the words he had just spoken. Any hope I had that he cared for me at the same level as Larry evaporated that night. My heart was broken.

Herb, Frances, and Dale, 1967

The man I admired most in the world had just told me, in his own way, that I wasn't equal to my brother in his eyes. We were finished as a father and son. I apologized and went into the bedroom Larry and I shared, closed the door, and went through the options of where I could go if I left the house for good that night. I knew I didn't want to stay there anymore, but I also realized that in the small town where everyone looked after each other's children, Daddy would make some excuse that I had run off after being punished, and they would just send me back for the three months of high school I had left.

I had no choice but to stay. But I resolved that the day I graduated high school would be the day I left Harlan and being under his roof. Regardless of how much I loved and admired him, I was determined to owe him as little as possible. Momma told me years later that, had I left, she would have gone with me. She admitted she was keenly aware of the different treatment and was equally devastated by the way he behaved that night. But as much as it hurt, it never impacted the reverence I had, and still have, for what he went through and the sacrifices he made for his country. Herbert "NMI" Hall was as true an American hero as any could be. In my sixties, I placed a brick at the World War II Museum in New Orleans in his honor and wished there was more I could do. I deeply respect and love him as my father and appreciate all he did to feed, clothe, and raise me as right as he could. But it would never be that we had the closeness of a father and son. We had our Harlan High School graduation on a Friday night in May 1967, and Saturday found me in Ohio staying with relatives and looking for a job. I would never return to Harlan to live again.

Aunt Rosalie and Uncle Theral Shepard lived in Ohio just outside Hamilton and allowed me to live with them over the summer of 1967 before I started at the University of Kentucky in the fall. I immediately got a job as a laborer at a homebuilding site working for one of their neighbors. My duties were to dig ditches, put tar waterproof on the concrete outside the basement, and any other menial jobs needed done. I embraced it with the zeal of someone who wanted to work. The pay was $1.50 per hour, but I could not have been happier. With blisters on my hands until I got a paycheck and could afford work gloves, I was working and paying my own way. I would give Theral and Rosalie part of my paycheck to cover my food expenses, but they wouldn't take anything for rent. Family took care of family. We had a wonderful summer, and I began to understand what it felt like to be on my own. I didn't have a car, but neither did I have enough money to go anywhere. It worked out fine.

Theral Shepard was quite a character. He loved to cut up and especially loved to pull pranks. He moved from job to job because of his alcoholism, but no man could have loved his family more. Alcoholism is a true disease, and alcohol was the drug of his generation. My generation had begun to get into the "drug scene," with the emergence of the hippie movement in California, but in the 1960s, no drugs would be found among the youth in eastern Kentucky except alcohol. Unfortunately, that would later change with the opioid "epidemic." The summer came and went with love and family gatherings. Larry and Judy Smithers eloped and moved near Middletown, Ohio, a common area for translocating from the hills of eastern Kentucky. Daddy was thrilled and Momma did all she could to help Judy.

My Mother and Father visited us once that summer, and I think Daddy was pleased to hear I was a hard worker that didn't shy away from any task that needed to be done. I always believed he thought because I liked learning and wanted to make a living with my mind, that I looked down on people who worked with their hands. It was far from true, but that didn't change things. Before I knew it, I was headed to Lexington and the University of Kentucky to start my college career and a new accomplishment for our family. If I was successful and graduated, I would be the first person in the history of our family to receive a bachelor's degree. However, the downside was I had no one to go to that could give me advice or guidance on how to adjust to and succeed at college. But I was anxious to begin.

CHAPTER 6:
Coming of Age

The University of Kentucky is a beautiful campus of over 800 acres. I had never seen anything so magnificent and overwhelming. The campus seemed much larger than the downtown area of Harlan, and I felt lost for the first time in my life. The hills of home could sometimes feel like a wilderness, but I never felt lost. UK was where Cotton Nash and Louie Dampier had played basketball under Coach Adolph Rupp, the Baron of Basketball. I would soon go to my first college football game! It was also the year the first African American, Nate Northington, played for the University of Kentucky. He played only a few minutes against Ole Miss before suffering a shoulder injury and leaving the game, but history was made. I was once again surprised by the opposition many students and alumni had for black people playing with white people, but times were changing. Some of the whites would joke, "He's not black, he's Puerto Rican!" After attending school at Harlan and getting to know wonderful black kids that had transferred from Rosenwald, I was struggling with why white people seemed so angry about having us go to school together.

But I also saw anger from black people on campus. UK had been upset in the national basketball tournament the year before by Texas Western, an all-black school. When I arrived on campus, there were protest marches at the basketball arena by black people holding signs and chanting, "Do it again, Texas Western, do it again." This, of course, irritated many white students on campus, and there were protests of the protests. The Reverend Martin Luther King Jr. had succeeded in obtaining social change through a strictly non-violent manner since he began the equal rights movement in the early 1960s, but there was still much to be done to change hearts on both sides of the issue.

The UK football team had never been anything to write home about since the departure of Paul "Bear" Bryant as head coach in the early 1950s. My freshman year of 1967 was no exception, with a record of two wins and eight losses, and one win and six losses in the southeastern conference. But I got to go to the games and, more important, actually see the players and coaches I had only read about, including Coach Rupp, the coach my father idolized. I attended a pep rally on campus before one of our football games and was standing near the stage. Through the crowd came the most inconspicuous, yet undeniable, Coach Adolph Rupp to say a few words. I was blown away by his size! I was no bigger than a popcorn fart, but this man was shorter than me! He couldn't have been more than 5 feet 6 inches tall but weighed about 175 pounds. When he talked, his multiple chins would cascade, and his jowls would constantly vibrate. Despite my awe for him, I had to laugh. But when this man started talking the world went silent. This was the master craftsman. No one challenged him as the Barron of Basketball. The 30 second shot clock was created because no one could stop his run and shoot offense, so opponents "froze" the ball to eat up the clock until they had a sure shot. Then Rupp's team would work the fast break he invented and score, usually within ten seconds. Then the slow pace would resume at the other end of the court. I remember time and again Daddy taking our small, white Motorola radio and plugging it in next to the pantry in the kitchen because that was the only place he could get a good signal at night. All so he could listen to his friend Cawood Ledford broadcast the UK basketball games. At halftime, he immediately walked the three or four steps to the telephone and called his brother-in-law, Ross, to complain about the officials or how the other team was "freezing the ball!"

I had made it! I was on the UK campus, and I had been within ten feet of Adolph Rupp!

The problem I faced in adjusting to college life was that I had no mentor or role model to advise or guide me through the things I suddenly needed to do on my own. My good friend, Homer Fortney, and his older brother, Bill Glenn, were there as friends, but I didn't understand my responsibilities as an adult on a campus that was so large the professors of your classes didn't know your name. I was walking across campus one morning on my way to class and heard someone yell, "Dale! Dale Hall!" Who in the world would I know in this mass of humanity? I turned to see a six-foot-four Lynn McGlothin, one of the older brothers of Jerry and Diane, my old neighbors. Lynn had just returned from his time in the Air Force and was back to school on the GI Bill. I was there on the GI Bill as well, because I was considered a war orphan due to my father's total disability. Otherwise, I could not have afforded to go to college. Lynn was just as happy to see a familiar face and, despite the seven years difference in our ages, we became fast friends. He taught me how to drink beer, enjoy life, and sow a few wild oats. We moved into a dorm room together at the beginning of the next semester. Unfortunately, because he was seven years my senior and had significantly matured while in the Air Force, I didn't pick up on the part about studying and going to class. I went to class some, but not nearly enough to learn what I needed to pass with a good grade. The professors at this large school could not be expected to know the names of 200 students in an auditorium taking English 101, and they certainly didn't take roll each class. It fell on me to be responsible, but I simply didn't know how at that point in my life. I was no longer under the control of my parents, nor in their debt, and all the inhibitions I had fostered in a Baptist home were let out of the box.

When I went home for Thanksgiving, I had to thumb from Lexington since I was without a car and Lynn was going to Louisville to visit Clay, his older brother. It felt like the longest trip of my life. I caught a ride easily enough out of Lexington on Interstate 75 that would take me to my exit at Corbin. It took me a couple of hours to get another ride to the Pineville bridge, where I would take Highway 421 to Loyall. But that was not so easy. By then it was dark, cold, and traffic was sparse on this old country road except for people driving home from work in Pineville. I had a couple of cars stop to ask where I was going, but they were only going a few miles and I would stand a better chance of getting a ride to Loyall if I stayed where I was. But after a couple of times turning down a ride, I made the mistake of getting in with some good folks that could take me about halfway. When they turned off the main road and I got out, I realized I was in the middle of nowhere and cars were flying by, afraid to pick someone up after dark.

About 1 a.m., I stuck out my thumb, duffle bag on the ground next to me, when an ambulance went by, slammed on the brakes, and backed up. The driver reached over and rolled down the window.

"Dale Hall, what the heck are you doing out here at this time of the night?"

It was Joe Mahan, whom I knew from Harlan and the proprietor at one of the funeral homes. I got in so fast it would make your head spin and said, "Joe, if I wasn't afraid you'd take it the wrong way, I'd kiss you right now!" Joe just laughed and said, "A handshake will do then." Joe was a kind and decent man who had delivered a corpse to the family a few hours away and was headed back home. He got me home a little before 2 a.m., and my mother was quickly up to unlock the door and greet me with a big hug. She had not slept knowing I was on my way home and knew I should have made it long before this. She was all too aware that the hills of eastern Kentucky can have bad elements. But I had made it home and she was relieved.

The next morning, she came into my bedroom when she heard me moving around about 10 a.m.

"Your Daddy is going to take you today to buy you a car to take to school. I don't want you to ever have to thumb to or back from school again."

"I appreciate the offer, Momma," I said, "but I like the idea of not owing him anything else. It makes me feel good. And if he buys me a car at this point, it will be out of guilt and you pushing him."

She replied, "I did tell him he had to do it after all the cars he bought Larry, but honey, please do this for me."

I continued to tell her I didn't want a car under these circumstances where I knew it wasn't Daddy's idea, but she pleaded.

"The money we have is half mine, and I have a right to spend money I've earned doing what Herb has done for Larry. Please do this for me," she said.

Tears were in her eyes, and I realized how much of an outsider she felt in the division that had been created in our small family. I finally agreed but admit it was clearly only because of all she had done for me. Daddy and I went to the car lot he chose. I asked, "What price do you want me to stay under?"

With a wave of his arm and some grit in his teeth, he said, "Any car on the lot. Pick whatever you want."

A new car at that time would have cost about $3,500, so I found one I knew would irritate him. It was an Oldsmobile convertible and was priced at $1,500. We had finally reached the point of truth between us. I knew he had no desire whatsoever to buy me a car but was forced to because of the multiple cars he had purchased either for or at the behest of my brother. He knew I was choosing a more expensive car than I needed for the same reason. I drove back to UK on Sunday with a convertible to drive around Lexington. To my knowledge, that was the last money I ever cost him except for food when I visited. I think with that transaction, we came to a silent acknowledgement of our relationship. The difference between us as individuals was simply too great.

Things didn't improve in my maturity when I went back for the second semester, and I enjoyed the spring running around with Lynn as much as I had the fall. Late at night on April 4, 1968, the television programs were interrupted with the news that Reverend Martin Luther

King, Jr. had been shot and killed while standing on his hotel balcony in Memphis, Tennessee. He was surrounded by Jesse Jackson and several other close associates, but nothing could be done. James Earl Ray was arrested shortly afterwards by Shelby County Sheriff Bill Morris, a man I would come to know later in my life. Much the same as his philosophical mentor Mahatma Gandhi had been killed by an assassin's bullet, this leader of equal rights for all met the same fate. Both killers were crazed radicals who could not tolerate the peaceful and loving teachings of their victims, nor could they cede their self-perceived position of superiority. Just over two months later, Robert F. Kennedy was assassinated by Sirhan Sirhan while campaigning for President at the Ambassador Hotel in Los Angeles. America was crying. While dreams of the future in the space program brought great hope in the '60s, the pain of hatred remained. America still had work to do to achieve her ideals.

At the end of two semesters, the University of Kentucky sent me a very nice letter telling me there was no need for me to return to campus the following fall. Apparently, they didn't think a 1.2 GPA was adequate to remain a student there. But when one door closes, another opens. Our local draft board had no such reservations about my GPA, IQ, or any other group of letters except 1A. No student deferment—report for induction into the Army. After my time with Lynn and his stories about the Air Force, I decided to show the draft board who was in charge and joined the Air Force for four years instead of being drafted for two years. The truth is, I didn't know if I had the intellectual foundation to get a college degree. I had no one to tell me, "Don't be ridiculous, just go to class and do your part by studying!" No one in my family had a college degree, and I didn't have the self-confidence. But I knew the Air Force would spend more time training me, hopefully in a trade I could use when I got out, and I could also get the GI Bill on my own for college or any kind of training I decided to pursue. I joined in May and was scheduled to report for induction in August.

Lynn and I got an apartment in Louisville for the summer, and each of us got jobs. I worked at a tool and dye factory running machines that sharpened saw blades. Just before I was scheduled to enlist in August, Momma called me to give me the bad news that my cousin, Philip New, Nita's eldest son, had been killed in Vietnam. I had lost a close cousin a few years earlier when Gary Colwell, Clarence's son, was killed in a car accident. I often went to visit Gary at their farm outside London, Kentucky during the summer and helped work the tobacco harvest and ride old Jim, the mule. Gary had a pony, so I rode the old razorback. It doesn't take long to learn why they're called razorbacks, but we built a makeshift saddle to give me some relief.

Philip and I were also close, and I spent a lot of time with him, Randy (Herbert's son), and Wallace Lee (Anna Lee's son) on our visits to Ohio. When I called Aunt Nita to offer my condolences, she told me the Major that delivered the somber news told her he could help delay my entry into the Air Force to allow me to attend Philip's funeral. But Philip's death made me want to seek revenge in whatever way I could and as soon as I could. Nita understood, and I declined the offer. On August 16, 1968 (three days before Daddy's 51st birthday), my mother and father drove me from Harlan to Louisville to be inducted into the Air Force. I signed the bill of sale for the Oldsmobile over to my father, thanked him, and told him I truly hoped he would be able to sell it and get most of his money back. I could tell he was genuinely proud that I was joining the Air Force. Perhaps he thought there might be hope for me yet. I boarded the bus with the other new recruits and headed for Lackland Air Force Base, Texas, for basic training.

CHAPTER 7:

The Air Force

We flew commercial as a group of from Louisville to San Antonio and arrived after dark. A crisply dressed sergeant walked on the blue Air Force bus we had boarded at the airport and immediately started spitting out commands in a loud, military voice. "No talking, no smoking, no chewing of gum. You are lower than the whale shit on the bottom of the ocean. You will do as you are told when you are told to do it!"

The military works to break everyone down, remove any sort of personal identity, and mold you into a part of a team. They're good at it. Over the next six weeks, I was called every name one can think of except those that referenced parents, race, or religion. Everything else was fair game. We were immediately hustled into a line to be officially mustered into the United States Air Force. For me, it was a mixture of pride and pure panic! The next morning, we had every semblance of hair removed from our heads, and within a few days were issued uniforms. Our name patches came later, and we sewed them above one breast pocket with "U.S. Air Force" above the other. The pride I felt when wearing the uniform of my country is hard to express. Those first days when we were without uniforms, all the different colored clothes made us look like a rainbow, and that's what new recruits are called. A Rainbow is the lowest in status, so we wanted to be in uniforms as quickly as we could! The willing loss of individual identity was quickly taking place.

Over the next six weeks, Flight 1027 learned how to dress, take care of personal hygiene (and some guys needed instruction!), march as a unit and, most important, when one of us broke a rule, the entire flight would suffer as if all had committed the sin. The only real treat I got while at Lackland was a visit with my cousin, Willard. Willard was the son of Dezzie and a career Air Force Tech Sergeant stationed at Lackland. He pulled some strings and I got to spend one Sunday with his family touring San Antonio. Then it was back to being lower than whale shit. By the time we graduated, we were a unit. Then, in true military fashion, we were split apart and sent to different Tech Schools to learn whatever craft the Air Force needed us to do. I was hoping for a trade that I could use after the Air Force, like jet engine mechanic or some other skill in the event I couldn't cut it at college. I was assigned to Keesler Air Force Base in Biloxi, Mississippi to be trained as a Morse Code Intercept Operator.

I wasn't sure what a Morse Code Intercept Operator did, but I hoped it was interesting and might support a living later on. We were housed in open bay barracks just as it was in basic training, but we had stand-up lockers that separated the bunks, and there was less of a rigid military approach. We were expected to maintain military discipline and march to and from class, chow, etc., but our free time was our own. I was assigned a bunk next to a guy named John Rice from Rome, Pennsylvania, and we became lifetime friends. I served as his best man when he married his beautiful wife, Linda. In Tech School, everyone called each other by their last names. It was easy to remember because we had them sewed above the pocket of our uniform. About a month into Tech School, someone noticed that John's name was Rice, not Ross. My Kentucky accent was so strong, and my "I's" so flat, they thought I was calling him Ross! Mrs. Hill would not have been proud of my diction.

On January 18, 1969, I received a message from the Officer of the Day at Keesler to report to his office. I went over to the Day Room and told the on-duty sergeant who I was and asked what it was all about.

"That's above my pay grade, son. The Captain will be with you shortly."

Soon after, I was directed to go into his office.

"Airman, there's no easy way to say this. We have been notified by the Red Cross that your father has passed away. I assume you will want to go home for the funeral, and we will assist in getting you there. I'm deeply sorry."

I was in shock but was able to get out a, "Thank you, Sir," and, "Yes, Sir, I would like to go home."

I called Mamma collect from a pay phone next to the barracks, and Nannie answered. In the 1960s, "long distance" phone calls were charged by the minute and you either dropped the appropriate coins into the phone slots or made the call "collect," meaning the receiving party accepted responsibility for the charges. Nannie told me that Daddy and Pop had been watching a University of Kentucky basketball game on TV when Daddy grabbed his chest and just laid over on the couch. He was dead instantly. The next 24 hours were a fog, but I remember flying on Delta in my dress blues from Biloxi to Knoxville, Tennessee, where my cousin, Jackie Lee; her husband, Bill; and their daughter, Beverly, met me and took me the rest of the way to Loyall. I was met at the door by Larry, with Momma close behind. Relatives and friends had already started to show up with food and comfort. In the hills, it is common for the body to lay in repose for viewing at the home, then taken to the church for the funeral and on to the cemetery. Harold Ball, an old friend of Daddy's and a mortician, was taking care of the body and preparing Herbert "NMI" Hall for his last journey. The next day, they brought him home, and he was there for visitation by friends and family until the funeral a day or so later. It was at the funeral that Daddy gave me the most important gift he could have ever given me.

The service was held at the First Baptist Church, next to the bridge I had fished under and walked across so many times growing up. Daddy didn't go to church after we moved to Loyall. He always said it was because the hard pews hurt his back and stomach, but I believe he held a silent anger that God had taken away the normal life he had always wanted. Nonetheless, he was a devout believer in God and never forgot his promise on the battlefield. When it was time for me to walk past him for my final goodbye before they closed the casket, I leaned over with tears running down my face and did what many hill folk did; I kissed him on the lips. A shock wave like I had never felt bolted through my body. I raised up, dry eyed and unemotional, and stared back down at the body that had been my father. He was cold and hard from the embalming, but it was translated in my mind that he had freed me from anything I might have owed him. He had already left this world and had given me the clear message that I was on my own for good. Instead of feeling emotions like anger or grief, I felt relief. I can't explain why. I suppose I felt he had said goodbye and sent me off to fulfill my life's mission, whatever that might be. I returned to Biloxi and finished my training with a new perspective on life and even more gratitude for all my father had done for me. We may not have ever been able to connect as individuals, but there was never a doubt about the love between us. It was simply different.

I knew from talking to Momma that government people had been interviewing my family and neighbors to find out what kind of person I was, but I didn't know why. I learned that the interviews being conducted were to determine if I could be trusted with classified information up to and including Top Secret. I must have passed because I was granted the highest clearance available, Top Secret Codeword. That meant the information was so current that a codeword was added each day to the classification of Top Secret that was stamped on the face of the document. If you didn't know the codeword, you were denied access to the information because you didn't have a "need to know." Upon completion of Tech School, I was a bonified Morse code operator and was ready to intercept whatever communications they needed. Since nearly all bases that housed our skill set were overseas, and the Air Force didn't care very much where we wanted to go, we got our assignments and prepared to leave, once again as individuals rather than a unit, to various bases across the globe.

We were sent to fill slots as they were needed wherever they were needed. I was assigned to Clark Air Force Base in the Philippines, Air Force Security Service, 6922nd Security Group. The Air Force police officers were called the Security Police, so I was somewhat confused about my role. But the SPs were under a totally different command. I was officially in that oxymoron, military intelligence. We were to intercept encrypted messages sent in Morse code by the Viet Cong, Cambodians, and Chinese, work with our code breakers to translate the messages, and share that with our on-the-ground commands to alert them of troop or supply shipment, air activity, or other valuable intelligence. We did this by using an R-390 radio built for its reliability and an AN/FLR-9 circularly disposed antenna array (CDAA). Also called a "flair-9," this omni directional antenna was so large it surrounded the entire compound. Because of the classified nature of our work and the curiosity of the locals and other troops, the antenna was dubbed the "elephant cage." This nickname was used all over the world at the bases from which the Security Service operated. When asked what that monstrosity was, we simply answered, "That's where we keep the elephants."

The FLR-9 "Elephant Cage"

Shortly after arriving at Clark, one of the most historic moments in human history occurred. President John F. Kennedy had laid down the challenge to America in 1962 to send a man to the moon and back by the end of the decade. On July 16, 1969, three American astronauts lifted off the launch pad at Kennedy Space Center for a historic flight to the moon. Neil Armstrong, Buzz Aldrin, and Michael Collins were the three chosen for the mission, with Armstrong as the commander and Collins as the pilot of the command module that would orbit the moon, while Armstrong and Aldrin took the lunar module "Eagle" to the surface. The 240,000-mile trip took 76 hours, and Apollo 11 reached the orbit of the moon on July 19, 1969. At 4:17 p.m. Eastern Standard Time on July 20, the craft touched down on the southwestern edge of what had been named the "Sea of Tranquility," and Armstrong transmitted the historic words back to earth: "The Eagle has landed."

At 10:39 p.m. EST, five hours ahead of schedule, Armstrong opened the hatch of the lunar module and began his descent to the surface. At

10:56 p.m. as Armstrong stepped off the ladder and became the first human to set foot on the surface of the moon, he uttered what is arguably the most profound statement ever made:

"That's one small step for a man, one giant leap for mankind."

Buzz Aldrin joined him on the surface 19 minutes later, and the two embarked on a two-hour mission to secure samples, take photographs, plant the American flag, and speak by phone via Houston to President Richard M. Nixon, who said it was the most historic phone call ever made from the White House. Among the items left on the moon was a plaque that read:

"Here men from the planet Earth first set foot on the moon, July 1969 A.D. We came in peace for all mankind."

There were five more successful lunar landing missions, and one unplanned lunar swing-by. Apollo 13 had to abort its lunar landing due to technical difficulties. The last men to walk on the moon, Astronauts Eugene Cernan and Harrison Schmidt of the Apollo 17 mission, left the lunar surface on December 14, 1972. For those of us in uniform, the Eagle landing was a very proud moment. But the Viet Cong were still on Earth, and our mission was here.

The military had not changed since my father's time, and it was simply required that my name be Henry D. Hall, instead of the H. Dale Hall I had used all my life. My parents didn't think about things like that when they named me Henry Dale and called me Dale. So, I became Henry and then Hank to all my Air Force buddies. They are the only ones that still call me Hank. Angeles City was just outside the gates of the base and was dominated by bars and bar girls. For a single man sowing his oats in life, it was more like heaven! My problem was I had still not matured enough to understand how to handle drinking. Over the next 16 months, I stayed more in a drunken mode than a sober one when off duty, but when we got to work, there was no question that we were very good at what we did. We didn't know it at the time, but the entire Security Service Command had been assigned to the National Security Agency (NSA), a civilian agency that didn't care whether our boots were polished if the critical information we gathered was accurate. The Air Force turned a blind eye to our MASH-like attitude towards military customs. What went on in the elephant cage stayed in the elephant cage.

Clark Field was the staging area for many of our troops going to Vietnam. The Army and Marines that would be going straight into the jungle were required to camp in tents on the base football field. I realized how fortunate I was to have that open bay barracks and a soft bunk to sleep in, as well as a Chow Hall and kitchen-prepared food. I respected my brothers in the other branches and thought of my cousin, Philip, when we were intercepting Charlie and helping shoot down planes or bomb ground troop or supply movements. I didn't know their names, but I wanted to do all I could to protect our brothers and sisters on the ground.

I was always pleased when I intercepted Charlie tracking a "friendly," one of his own aircraft. When we got the codes for a friendly, we immediately notified the Direction-Finding unit, and they would shoot coordinates on where the plane was and which direction it was going. One of the true rewards of a maddening job listening to atmospheric blasts that were literally painful to your eardrums and the endless *dits* and *dahs* for hours was getting the code from Charlie that the friendly we had been tracking had been shot down by "hostile" aircraft. Mission accomplished! We never knew how many American troop lives had been saved, but we knew some were, and that was enough. Occasionally, the effort was highly significant, and we would receive a commendation for our work. The officers would come into our work area, read the commendation, thank us, and tell us that's the last time we would ever see it because it was classified. Upon discharge, I received my basic military records, but there was never a mention of commendations. We were the Silent Service, and the intel we intercepted was regularly included in the morning security briefing for the President of the United States. Not bad for grunts that worked in an elephant cage.

I knew my father's death was working on my mother, who was only 42 at the time. I got letters from her saying she was at the grave in a rocking chair visiting with Herb. For a kid who was still dealing with growing up and no phones to talk live with her for 16 months, it was hard to take. I talked privately with our lieutenant but quickly realized he was only three or four years older than me. I went to the Base Exchange and bought two portable tape recorders that we could use to send each other taped messages. I recorded the first message and included it in her recorder with another blank tape, along with instructions on how to use it. It made things better to hear each other's voices but didn't fix the problem. I kept telling her it was okay to get on with her life and not to "rock your damned life away next to a grave." I purposely used a word she would never use to drive home the point and hopefully have her snap out of it. It apparently worked.

One of the couples who lived near the Farmers up Cedar Street was Leland and Ruby Martin. We knew them as good people. Leland couldn't have children, but they raised Ruby's brother, Bobby, as their own. Ruby passed away when I was in Tech School and, by the time I was in the Philippines, Momma had struck up a friendship with Leland through church and the mutual grief of losing their spouses. Nature took its course, and they started seeing each other. When she asked me in one of the tapes if I thought it was okay for her to see Leland, I responded as quickly as I could that I absolutely approved. But I also reminded her that she had been a loving and faithful wife to Daddy for over 24 years and needed neither mine *nor* Larry's approval. She had earned the right to find happiness.

Not too long afterwards, she let me know they had married. I was happy for her. Larry was not. I had underestimated the bond he had with Daddy but was still shocked at the meanness he showed her for not giving up life at 42 years of age. He did all he could to make her feel cheap for finding another husband, but I continually told her it was none of his or my business and she should be happy. I believe she was, and I know Leland treated her with dignity and respect. This behavior was not new to Larry. He had sought, and been given, very special treatment from Daddy, and he expected the same from Momma. I finally had to let him know that, if necessary, we could meet face to face and physically settle the argument, but he was not to be disrespectful to my mother again. Things settled down after that, but Larry broke off communications with Momma until Leland died.

My next assignment would undoubtedly be overseas, so I volunteered for Vietnam. I was beginning to think about money when I got out, and Vietnam duty was exempt from taxes, and you received combat pay. At twenty, dying is not something you believe will happen to you. But the Air Force and the spiritual hand that was guiding my life had a different plan, and I was assigned to Brindisi, Italy for my second tour. When my 16 months in the Philippines was over and I flew back home, we went by military charter from the Philippines to Japan, then on to Travis Air Force Base outside San Francisco. We were all in uniform and extremely tired from the nearly 24-hour trip when we were bussed from Travis to San Francisco International Airport.

I had tickets on American Airlines, and the bus let me off at the door leading to the ticket counter. It was less than 50 yards to the counter, but I was spit at and called a fascist baby killer twice before I could make it from the door to the counter. America was divided over the war, and those of us who were simply trying to serve our country became the easy target of the protesters. None of us in uniform during the Vietnam War ever heard the words, "Thank you for your service and welcome home." So be it. We didn't serve to receive thanks. We proudly served because it was our duty. No one will ever take that pride from us.

I had volunteered for Vietnam only to be assigned to Italy, but Russ Mullen, one of my good friends in the Philippines, was assigned to Vietnam airborne. Airborne for us meant flying around in a slow-moving EC-47 "Gooney Bird" aircraft below 12,000 feet, monitoring Charlie and being an easy target. Russ's plane was shot down, and he was held as a prisoner of war for a time before he was able to escape. I thank God my Air Force Brother was able to survive. It was no game. I was assigned to Italy to spy on Ivan the Soviet instead. But I was becoming more and more aware of the hand guiding my life. I wasn't sure what it was, but knew it wasn't of this world.

San Vito dei Normanni Air Station was located outside Brindisi and was different than the Philippines in almost every way. There was true normalcy there. The towns outside the base weren't set up to cater to the GI. They were Italian towns with centuries of their own traditions and norms. Brindisi is located in the heel of the boot in southern Italy, the ultra-conservative part of the country, and more tied to the old ways of Sicily than the modern Florence in its traditions. In my whole time there, I never took an Italian girl out on a date because to do so would require her entire family to accompany the couple. That wasn't going to happen. Our way to meet girls was through the tourists that came to Brindisi to catch the ferry boat to Corfu and other Greek islands.

San Vito also allowed guys to have their wives and families there with them. I hadn't realized how socially isolated we were from normal life in the Philippines until I got to Brindisi. Tom Lear, Ken Will, and Mike Mesi had been in the Philippines with me and were also assigned to San Vito. Because we were now all Sergeants (E-4), we were allowed to live off base and receive food ration pay instead of eating at the Chow Hall. Ken, Tom, a neat guy we met named Brad Cooper, and I went together and rented a villa outside Brindisi. Of course we needed to name the Villa, so we assigned that to Brad. Brad was constantly coming up with jokes, so we allowed him to name it Huntley Manor, after a childhood friend of his. Huntley Manor soon became one of the places to congregate for everyone in their off-duty time. Some wonderful wives were great additions who made us all feel like we had sisters in the house, as well as the cute girls that would consent to visit with us from the boats. Rich and Linny Wells were from Nebraska, and Ed and Linda Kostro (we called him Fidel for obvious reasons) were from Chicago and always a joy to have around. Our Boston buddy, Bill DiRosario, met his future wife, Kerrie, there, an Australian traveling through Europe. These folks and others like Dave Incorvati, Tom Whatley, Bob Locke, Jimmy Hodges, Pete Weeks, Monty Garner, and Lynn Kelch became our family away from home and have remained so for life.

Our work schedule consisted of rotating shifts, or flights, and we were on Dawg Flight. That meant we worked four days from 4 p.m. to midnight, came in the next night at midnight and worked four days from midnight until 7 a.m., and then came in at 7 a.m. the next morning and worked until 4 p.m. for four days. Then it was party time! When we got off at 4 p.m. on the fourth day, we were off until 4 p.m. four days later! That allowed us to take off and see Italy or, on occasion, take the ferry boat to the Greek Island of Corfu. The wives would always accompany us, and it was like a family outing each time that happened. We didn't receive the gratification of helping shoot down aircraft from the Soviet Union, but we were compensated with family instead. It's a strange and powerful bond that unites people who serve their country together. Unless you are counted in the less than 7% of Americans who have worn our nation's uniform and written a blank check up to and including your life, it's difficult to grasp. But patriotism runs deep. While we joked and talked constantly about what we were going to do when we got out, we were proud to be doing our part for our country. I would still give my life for any of them.

While in Italy, I began to slowly build my self-confidence about college and my ability to return and be capable of success. Many of the guys with whom I served had either completed college or had at least one year, and they scoffed at the idea that I would not be able to make it. Captain Larry Banister once answered my question by saying, "You have seen things few in the world have seen. The good and the bad. You have drunk enough beer to float a battleship. The only thing you have left to prove is to yourself. You'll do fine in college."

I took his words to heart and started thinking about what I wanted to study when I got out. The GI Bill gave me one month of education benefits for every month I served active duty, which could be up to 48 months.

I started having problems with one of my molars while at San Vito and needed to see the base dentist. At my appointment, I was introduced to a young Captain just out of dental school with lots of good ideas about saving teeth instead of just extracting them. He asked if I would let him try to re-build the roots of my bad tooth and put it back in with a splint to hold it until the new roots attached to the new tissue? I, of course, said yes and was fascinated by the idea of doing innovative things like this. My only experience with a dentist had come with much pain and suffering when I broke a front tooth as a child and had to have a root canal. Back then, going to the dentist was one of the worst fears a child could have. To be exposed to someone that seemed excited about fixing my tooth struck a chord, and I began to think about dentistry as my future profession. The more I thought about it, the more convinced I became. I would be a dentist. The experiment, however, didn't go so well. I still occasionally got drunk and spit out the splint. He put a bridge in instead.

Another lifechanging event was when I started studying Karate. I had begun in the Philippines but hadn't taken it too seriously. In Italy, however, we didn't have much to do after our shifts, so I started looking at possible hobbies. Sandy Orsetti was on Dawg Flight with us and was deeply committed to the Martial Arts. The thing that changed my whole view of Karate was the approach Sandy took. It wasn't about breaking boards or becoming some badass, even though the capability was there. Nor was it a hobby. It was about spirituality and growth of one's soul. I had never been attracted to religions because every one of them seemed to say all the others were going to hell and that they were the only true believers. But I always believed in the Creator of my grandfather's "nadur" and knew there was a greater force in the universe that had provided us the blessings of life.

Karate, as invented by Monks, was used to gain control over one's body through the mind and have the body do things that went beyond what was thought possible. True Karate teaches that violence is the *last* resort, and self-restraint is victory. It doesn't matter if the guy trying to bully you thinks you're afraid of him, as long as you aren't forced to hurt him. But if given no choice, it teaches to do it quickly, and be humble about one's abilities. It would be a sin for someone knowledgeable in Karate to initiate conflict.

That would signal an inability to control impulses and dishonor the spirituality that should guide all our thoughts and actions. It is through meditation that I became deeply connected with my Creator and began the journey of understanding all He has given us. That is why I am so awed by sunrises. To me, the Creator has given me another day of opportunities to enjoy His gifts and do my part to make life better for others. Karate also gave me the confidence to know I could succeed in college if I dedicated my efforts to graduating. Throughout my professional career, the lessons I learned from Karate taught me to take a deep breath, remain calm, and extract the facts from an emotional issue without fear.

About a year after my arrival, I was sitting at my station inside the compound copying Ivan, and someone walked by, patted me on the shoulder, and said, "Congratulations, Sergeant!"

I made some snide comment because we didn't practice military protocol in the compound.

He said, "You need to go check the promotion list."

I thought he was joking, but I got up and went back to see my name on the list to be promoted to Staff Sergeant (E-5). I was more shocked than anyone because only a small percentage of Sergeants got promoted to E-5 in their first four years, and I was probably one of the least deserving. Welcome to military logic. Our time passed at San Vito, and soon enough it was April 1972. My assigned time of 18 months for this tour was ending, but my full four-year obligation lasted another month. As expected, my tour was extended to complete my four-year obligation. I got my discharge orders and, after 19 months in Italy, was mustered out of the Air Force at Fort Dix, New Jersey on May 19, 1972, with an Honorable Discharge. According to my DD214, the official document of military service, I had served my country for four years and four days. It was time to get my education wagon back in gear, take advantage of the GI Bill education benefits I had earned, and set my sights on a pre-Dental degree in Biology and Chemistry. I was ready and raring to go! Time had been lost, and I wanted to make it up as fast as I could.

At 22 with my Air Force years behind me, I was finally mature enough to know not to run full bore into the heavy challenges of college. I had experienced the cold nature of classes with hundreds of students and knew I needed the insurance policy of at least having the professor know my name. I ran into Homer Fortney in Harlan almost as soon as I returned home. We had both received letters from UK four years earlier; mine was "don't come back," while his was probation. He elected to go to Cumberland College, a smaller school in southern Kentucky not far from Harlan. It was a private Baptist college, and the entire enrollment at that time was around 1,500. He told me it really helped him get his focus back and recommended I go there at least for the summer semesters. He, too, had decided to be a dentist and had recently been accepted at the University of Louisville School of Dentistry. Since Homer's path had seemed so close to mine and had worked well for him, I took his advice and immediately enrolled at this small college in Williamsburg for the summer semesters. I was back in school in less than a month after my discharge from the Air Force.

My Appalachian Trail

On June 17, 1972, five men broke into the headquarters of the Democratic National Committee to gain information on strategy for the upcoming election between President Richard Nixon and Walter Mondale. Soon after, they were arrested and one of the greatest political scandals of the 20th century began to unfold. These five men were later connected to the White House and the Nixon campaign. Over the fall and winter months, significant activity in Congress relative to the jurisdiction of House and Senate Oversight Committees culminated in the Senate creating a special investigative committee to look into the issues. For the first time in history, the hearings were covered in the national media from gavel to gavel. Senators heard testimony that the President of the United States had personally approved plans to cover up his Administration's involvement with the Watergate break-in and learned of the existence of a voice-activated taping system in the Oval Office.

America was captivated by the up close and personal witnessing of our government in action. Few had ever seen a Congressional hearing, and none had witnessed testimony that tied a sitting president to criminal activities. The results of the hearings were turned over to the leadership of the House and Senate. In February 1974, the U.S. House of Representatives began Impeachment deliberations against the President of the United States of America for only the second time in history. On July 24, the Supreme Court ordered President Richard Nixon to release all tapes of conversations in the Oval Office. This ruling changed the course of history and exposed the crushing truth about politics and power in a way never before so openly seen in America.

With the outcome of the proceedings becoming clearer with each review of the tapes, President Richard Milhouse Nixon resigned on August 9, 1974. Altogether, the scandal resulted in the indictments of 69 people with 48 ultimately found guilty. Vice President Spiro Agnew had already resigned from office due to other potential shenanigans, leaving former Speaker of the House Gerald Ford as Vice President. With the resignation of President Nixon, Gerald R. Ford became President of the United States of America under the dictates of the Constitution. President Ford nominated Nelson Rockefeller as Vice President of the United States, and the Senate and House confirmed him under the terms of the 25th Amendment to the Constitution. In an apparent effort to heal the nation, President Ford pardoned Richard Nixon on September 8, shortly after taking office. That would come back to haunt him.

CHAPTER 8:

Back to College

Leland loved to fool around trading used cars, and he gave me a 1967 Chevy Malibu as a "coming home" gift. He was a good-hearted man, and I believe he somehow felt he owed me for supporting his marriage to Momma in the face of Larry's opposition. I told him he didn't owe me any thanks and that all I wanted was for Momma to be happy. I believed she was. Still, they both wanted me to have the car, and it saved me from having to use money I had put aside in the Air Force for my education. I also think Momma felt I was owed a car to replace the Oldsmobile I gave back to Daddy when I went in the Air Force. The GI Bill gave me enough help to cover tuition and much of room and board, but I still had to work odd jobs to cover books and the rest of my bills. The car was a big help.

I didn't have a lot of extra money, and there were times I had very little food in the cupboard. I was by no means alone in the poverty of students that had come from Appalachia trying to better their lives. Sometimes, late in the month before the next GI Bill check arrived, I had to mix ketchup with water to have tomato juice for breakfast. I was proud and wouldn't let Momma and Leland help me with money or groceries. I believed the time had passed when they should be helping to support me. But when I visited Loyall for the occasional weekend, I often found a twenty-dollar bill hidden in my ashtray or behind the sun visor when I got back to school. It made her feel good to help, and I knew she needed to do something.

A break came my way when I became acquainted with my professor of Anatomy and Physiology. Dr. Jerry Davis was a headstrong academic that accepted no nonsense and expected you to learn the material. He told me I was one of the best students in his class and he still gave me a B! After that semester, he asked me if I would help him put together a lab book for Anatomy and Physiology specifically for nurses, a program he was about to initiate at Cumberland. Not only would I get to spend more time picking his brain about how the human body works, but also he would pay me to do it! After completion of the lab book, he asked me to teach the lab to the new class of nurses. This professor that I held in such high esteem had given me a tremendous boost of confidence. He had no idea how much that helped me believe in myself and gain the determination to keep moving forward. Dr. Davis went on to be the President of Alice Lloyd College in Kentucky, and then President of College of the Ozarks in Branson, Missouri, also known as Hard Work U, where all students work and no one pays tuition. His commitment to excellence and belief in the teachings of his Creator changed the lives of many, many students. Not just mine. I have always held Jerry Davis as an example of what higher education is all about: helping unsure students believe in themselves.

A significant aspect of dentistry I wanted to understand was how it worked in real life. Mrs. Alder, a nurse that lived in the trailer court where I rented, offered to introduce me to a well-known dentist in Williamsburg and a top graduate of the University of Kentucky dental school. She made the phone call and set up the time for me to go by his office. I arrived about 15 minutes before my appointment, introduced myself to the receptionist, and said I'd like to visit with Dr. West. I told her I was pre-dental and wanted to know what it was really like being a dentist, and he had agreed to see me.

She excused herself, and in about ten minutes, a man with curly brown hair, slightly orange-shaded glasses, and a wide grin walked out into the waiting area and asked me to follow him. We went out on the small porch stoop he had at the back of his office where he commenced to take out a few fingers of Red Man chewing tobacco and stuff it into his cheek. Then with a grin, he said, "I hear you're planning to be a dentist."

I said, "Yes, Sir. I have been through the Air Force and have learned enough to know that nothing is really what it appears on the surface. If you'll let me watch you work and learn what dentistry is really like, I'll empty your trash, wash your car, do whatever you need done around here, and I ask no pay."

He was so struck by my desire to see the whole story that he immediately said, "Absolutely! I'd love to have you around here. I'll show you how to make crowns and bridges too. And I'll pay you."

"That's wonderful, Sir. But I can't take pay. What I'll learn is likely more than I could ever afford to buy."

Dr. Bob West and I became immediate friends.

I met his beautiful wife, Jenny Lou, and their sons, Bobby and Larry, as they started treating me as part of their family. But I sadly learned that Bob was an alcoholic and a man that just seemed unhappy with his life, even though he was hailed by the Dean of the UK Dental school as a star graduate, had a beautiful wife, and two wonderful sons. Dentistry in the 1960s and 1970s had the highest rates of alcoholism and suicide of any medical profession. It made sense once I remembered the dread I felt when going to the dentist in the Air Force based on my experience as a child. People at that time simply didn't want to go to the dentist. One day, I was watching Bob work, and he suddenly pushed back from the patient and said, "Get on up and out of here. I can't work on a moving target, and you won't be still so I can do my work!"

The patient said, "But, Doc, I'm afraid it's gonna hurt!" That summed it up. Even though he was exceptional at what he did, he felt no gratification because the people he was helping only wanted to get it over with. He began regularly telling me that I would not be happy as a dentist, and I should think about doing something else. But I was determined.

Bob accepted my determination and set up a meeting with Dr. Alvin Morris, Dean of Dentistry at the University of Kentucky. We drove the two hours to Lexington one afternoon when Bob's office was closed and made it to the Dean's office around 4:30. Dr. Morris was a true gentleman and treated me as if I were someone special as he bragged about his star student. He asked me a few questions and found out I was an Air Force veteran. I could tell he held that experience in high regard. I was honest with him about my first year's academic record but that I had nothing less than a 3.6 GPA since my return to college. After we finished visiting, he instructed me to send my application for dental school to his office and he would see that it got proper consideration. I was on cloud nine all the way back to Williamsburg, and I could tell Bob had been reminded of his achievements and seemed to regain a sense of pride.

I managed to find a girlfriend while at Cumberland, Linda Mitchell from Barbourville, a town about halfway between Williamsburg and Harlan. I learned a hard lesson with her mother about the unhappiness that can come when parents try to control the lives of their children. Her mother ultimately drove us apart. Linda went home each weekend to be with her parents, and I would very often go be with Bob and Jenny Lou at their 300-acre farm just outside Williamsburg. They had horses and would let me ride around the farm just enjoying things I couldn't afford at that time. They were wonderful friends.

I applied for dental school in my "last year," although my undergraduate work didn't follow the normal schedule. When I got out of the Air Force, I felt as if I had four years to make up in a short period of time. Starting in May 1972, I took all the hours they would allow me to take in both summer semesters and both full term semesters. As a result, I graduated with a Bachelor of Science degree in August 1974 after only 27 months, while also retaking many of the courses I failed the first year. My Cumberland GPA was now about 3.6 but was pulled down to 3.2 because of the first year at UK. That proved costly.

When I got my letter notifying me of the new class for Dental School, there were 90 people selected to be in the class. I was not one of them. I was on the alternate list of 5 in case any of those selected decided to go to another dental school. In 1974, the University of Kentucky was elevated to the number two dental school in the nation by the American Dental Association and, not surprising, no one selected for the class declined admission. I was paying the price for that first year. In another envelope was a letter from Dean Morris. It was very cordial and let me know that he would ensure I got in next year if I went on to graduate school and took classes that could transfer in-state at the graduate level.

I sucked it up, accepted ownership of my earlier behavior and academic record and enrolled at Eastern Kentucky University graduate school of Biological Sciences under Department Head Dr. Edwin Hess, with Dr. John Williams as my major professor. John Williams was an ex-State Trooper who took no BS but could occasionally spread some. I loved him! He immediately took me under his wing and started telling me how I needed to forget the dentistry stuff and go into fisheries biology like I was intended to do! He had one daughter and no sons, so all of us graduate student guys were his sons and were proud to be so. As the year went on, I realized that the study I was doing on newly formed Cave Run Lake near Moorhead would easily satisfy the research requirements and, along with the adequate number of class hours I would complete, end up allowing me to get a master's degree in Limnology. I unrealistically thought I could write my thesis while in dental school and make the best use of a delayed year. But then it happened.

As head of the Department of Biological Sciences, Dr. Hess controlled all the purse strings and had to approve all purchases. One of the critical pieces of equipment for my research was a depth sensitive photometer, an instrument to measure the penetration of light in the water at various depths. This would help me understand the depth to which light-dependent plankton would be able to survive and would help describe the new lake's biological structure. I was not aware of anyone else using this piece of equipment in their research, but when I went to get it for a day of sample collection, I found it broken! It almost appeared to have been hit with a sledgehammer, but more likely someone knocked it off the shelf getting something else and refused to take responsibility. I could not finish my remaining, and necessary, summer months of field research to show an entire year of biological variation without this equipment. Dr. Hess would have to approve the purchase of a new one.

Dr. Williams went to Dr. Hess to ask for the new equipment and was flatly denied.

"What? Are you just going to leave this young man hanging when he did nothing? He has already finished the coursework and needs this piece of equipment, or he has to start all over!"

Hess said, "I don't care. I'm not spending hundreds of dollars on a piece of equipment that doesn't get used that much. He can just start over."

John Williams stormed out of his office and had to go calm down to keep "Trooper Williams" from breaking Hess' "shitty pencil neck!" (Williams 1975)

I was screwed. Just when I thought things had come together and I would not only be going to Dental School but would also have a master's degree, the door slammed shut. By this time, I had learned to listen closely to the subliminal message that was being delivered by the hand that was guiding me, and it was clear that a new path was being directed. I have no doubt Dean Morris would have kept his promise and helped me get into the UK Dental School, but between Bob and John both telling me I would not be happy as a dentist, and another stomach punch from the invisible force, I decided to pick myself up and start all over. I was being somehow compelled, and even more determined, to get up and move on with my education. Quitting was not an option.

Dr. Edwin Hess had clearly demonstrated how some "professors" and schools treat their students. Tough luck, you're on your own. I believed then, and I believe now, that Edwin Hess had no business whatsoever being in charge of other peoples' lives. He had neither the leadership skills nor the attitude to achieve success in his responsibilities. Dr. Williams, on the other hand, quickly started calling former colleagues and students who were now professors to tell them the story of this young man that had just been screwed by an uncaring Department head.

He found one in Dr. Fred Bryan, a professor and head of the Cooperative Fisheries Research Unit of the U.S. Fish and Wildlife Service (FWS), located on the Louisiana State University (LSU) campus. When Dr. Bryan heard the story, he said, "Send him down right away. I'll give him a position as a graduate assistant if he is willing to work on the early life history of fish."

In contrast to Edwin Hess, Fred Bryan accepted a graduate student, sight unseen, based solely on the story he heard and the recommendation of his friend. I will forever be grateful to John Williams and Fred Bryan, two professionals who developed young lives and careers, and to the Louisiana State University that welcomed me.

Just as one door closed on a school that seemed to care only for the bottom line, another door opened with an Academic Institution that was dedicated to building lives. I was committed to follow this journey and, if knocked down, get back up and keep going no matter how many times it took. As doors closed and opened, I learned to listen to the message I was receiving from the people that would lead me to my destiny. To this day, I thank Dr. Morris for his willingness to help get me into dental school, but I believe the architect of my life had other plans for my future. I was off to Louisiana, LSU and a new beginning.

CHAPTER 9:
LSU and My New Family

In May 1975, I rented a U-Haul trailer, filled it with my meager belongings, and headed from Richmond, Kentucky to Baton Rouge, Louisiana. I had no idea what to expect. I knew of Louisiana through the stories of the deep south from Bob Locke, Jerry Zeringue, and some of my Louisiana buddies in the Air Force but had never been there. Biloxi and Keesler AFB were close, but a totally different culture. I remember as I came down Interstate 55 and took a right turn on to I-12 West how struck I was by the flat and open topography. Dr. Bryan had told me I would be working in the Atchafalaya Basin, but it sounded like "Chaf-fly" when everyone said it. It certainly didn't seem to be pronounced like its spelling, but this was Cajun country and the French, Spanish, Native American, and Caribbean influence made the language unique. I learned it was pronounced At-chaf-uh-ly-uh and was immediately dubbed a Yankee, a term not deemed a compliment, because I struggled with its pronunciation.

The two major rivers that empty into Louisiana's Gulf Coast are the Mississippi and the Atchafalaya. As the Mississippi River drains 42% of the continental U.S., that means a lot of water passes by Baton Rouge and New Orleans on its way to the Gulf. The Atchafalaya is formed by a diversion from the Mississippi River (Old River Control Structure) north of Baton Rouge near Vidalia, and the Louisiana Red River. The Lower Mississippi Alluvial Valley was sculpted by constantly changing rivers whose new courses cut new channels, built natural alluvial berms through flooding, and carried the rich alluvial soils that built the most productive forested wetlands and coastal marshes in the world. Without the pressure-relieving diversion of Mississippi River water, the Mississippi would once again change course and move to the west, with the devastating effects of flooding down the Atchafalaya and leaving Ports of national significance in Baton Rouge and New Orleans high and dry.

The U.S. Army Corps of Engineers (Corps) operates the Old River Control Structure and is charged with seeing that the Mississippi does not change course. This is done by diverting approximately 30% of the Mississippi River flow through a seven-mile channel to join with the Red River near Simmesport, Louisiana, and form the Atchafalaya River. The Corps is also responsible for overseeing and permitting water dependent development along the Atchafalaya, and to understand what impacts that development might have on the lifeforms of the river. That is where I came in.

Fred Bryan was the Unit Leader for the LSU Cooperative Fisheries Research Unit, a partnership office between the U.S. Fish and Wildlife Service (FWS), Louisiana Department of Wildlife and Fisheries, and LSU.

The Co-op Unit Program had earned high respect throughout the country for excellent science and strong partnerships. As counterparts to the Fisheries Units, there were also Cooperative Wildlife Research Units at Universities across the nation. The Unit Leaders were employees in the FWS' Research Region and were usually GS-13/14. Fred wanted me to study the fishes of the Atchafalaya and document when they spawned, where they spawned, and how they were recruited into the river populations. The field of focus is called Early Life History and has the technical name of Ichthyoplanktology (Ick-thee-o-plank-tol-o-gee). My thesis work required collecting samples of eggs and larvae of fishes from the floodplains of the river and backwater bayous and was titled: *The Spatial and Temporal Distribution of Ichthyoplankton of the Upper Atchafalaya Basin.*

This research would hopefully enable all parties to assess the impacts of various drainage and development projects along the Atchafalaya, but also to understand how fishes behave in other warm, freshwater environments. I had never heard of this discipline of study, but it sounded interesting. I was ready to start anew. A not too well-understood aspect of advanced degrees in science (Master of Science or Doctor of Philosophy) is that in order to achieve the distinction, one must *increase* the knowledge base of their field through research presented in a thesis or Dissertation, and *defend* that science to a board of professors at the University. Until this is accomplished, the title of M.S. or PhD cannot be achieved. The PhD student who has succeeded in making this contribution of increased knowledge in her/his field is the true *Doctor*, not simply learning what others have done, but providing new information to inform future analyses. I mean no disrespect to physicians, dentists, and others who are practitioners, but I believe it is appropriate to recognize this important distinction.

Nelson Horseman had been a fellow graduate student under Dr. Williams at Eastern Kentucky University and was working on his PhD with Dr. Bryan at LSU, which gave me at least a small anchor from home to seek advice. He proved to be a good friend and was instrumental in my transition. Nelson helped me find an apartment on Burgin Street, not far from campus. The graduate assistantship not only paid for my tuition but gave me a monthly stipend of a few hundred dollars! This, along with the GI Bill, allowed me to focus entirely on my studies and not have to seek side jobs. Fred Bryan was treating me with every courtesy he promised, and I was not about to let him down.

Momma, being the good Christian woman she was, just couldn't hold it in that she was worried about me living on that famous Burgin Street! I had to carefully educate her that the street for which she had so much concern was Bourbon Street, and it was in New Orleans, not Baton Rouge. She was somewhat reassured by this, but I think she always kept that finger pointed at me to behave myself. At least, I felt it.

The Burgin apartment was short-term, and I found another apartment that put me almost on campus and near the Parker Agricultural Center, also known as the Cow Palace, where my graduate student office was located under the bleachers of the livestock arena. My new apartment was on Earl Gros (pronounced Grow) and had a nice pool with good neighbors. One of those neighbors was a newlywed couple named Frank and Trelle Blackburn. Frank was a Louisiana State Police trooper, and Trelle was an elementary school teacher. Once Frank learned I was an Air Force veteran, this Marine and I became good friends. Trelle was a beautiful, outgoing girl who never met a stranger and treated everyone she met as a lifelong friend. Frank's trooper friend, Ronnie Jones, and his wife, Weezie (Louise), came by often, and I became friends with them as well. Weezie was studying Microbiology at the graduate level and focusing on pathological agents. She eventually received her advanced degree and went to work with the U.S. Center for Disease Control and Prevention. In 1998, Mary Louise Martin was among those killed in the Nairobi Embassy bombing.

One day in June, I went down to the pool after returning from school and ran into one of the most beautiful girls I had ever seen. She had an hourglass figure, long black hair down past her shoulder blades, olive-tanned skin, and dark brown eyes that displayed her Cajun heritage. I introduced myself and discovered she had been Trelle's college roommate and best friend. Sarah Virginia Reed was from Bunkie, a small town in central Louisiana that was heavy into farming. Her father grew soybeans, but often rotated crops to take advantage of commodity price shifts. Sarah had just finished her master's degree in education and was employed as a state social worker across the Mississippi River in Plaquemines, Louisiana. In the course of the conversation, I asked if she was seeing anyone. I was simply not going to let this opportunity pass without at least a try. When she said no, I said, "Maybe we can take in a flick sometime?" She said that sounded good, and I headed up to my apartment after getting her phone number.

A day or two later, I called Sarah and asked her to go with me to see the new movie *Jaws*, a thriller about a killer shark that seemed to have a calculating mind much like Moby Dick. I had my first date with the girl I would fall in love with and marry. I didn't know it at the time, nor did she, but our previous failed romances had taught us both to find not only love, but the depth of a loving relationship regardless of family issues. Sarah had recently broken up with her high school sweetheart because he would not oppose his father and marry a catholic. She had also learned firsthand the damage interfering parents could inflict. A month or two later, Sarah asked me to go home with her one weekend and meet her parents. I knew this meant she had developed strong feelings for me as well, and I was ready to learn more about her family and the environment that molded her.

As we pulled into her driveway a little after dark and headed to the door of her family home, we were met at the door by a man with a big grin, holding out his hand, saying, "Hello. I'm Herman Reed. Would you like a beer or a highball?" These were people I would like. Not only did I come to love both Herman and his wonderful wife, Nell, but also I came to see them as my second parents. Herman was a WWII Army veteran of the European Campaign, and very proud of his service. Nell was the epitome of the beautiful Cajun woman; dark hair, gracious host, and a wonderful cook! Nell and Momma became wonderful long-distance friends. As time would prove, neither Herman nor Nell ever attempted to interfere in any way with Sarah and my relationship or decisions.

Sarah had two sisters and one brother. Fernell, Sarah's older sister, and her husband, Richard Cryar, had a daughter, Mary Katherine, and twin boys, Ian and Christopher. They lived in Morgan City, Louisiana, and Richard worked for Leevac Marine as an accountant. Fernell was a stay-at-home mom and had her hands full with three little ones. Phyllis, Sarah's younger sister, was a physical therapist and flight attendant for Eastern Air Lines. She was home based in San Juan, Puerto Rico and got home as often as she could. Melvin was Sarah's only brother and had just graduated High School when I first went to Bunkie. The whole family was wonderful and made me feel as if I had known them my entire life. If it didn't work out between Sarah and me, at least I knew it would not be because of domineering parents or interfering siblings.

Herman and Nell Reed, 1947

I felt at home with Herman and became closer to him than I ever had my own father. Herman was a character. He made light of his trek across Europe fighting the Nazis but was fiercely proud of his service. Just as was the case with my father. Herman Reed took no quarter and gave none. He was as giving as anyone you ever met, even to strangers, but it would not have been wise to disrespect him. One evening when we were visiting, a young woman and her little girl knocked on the door of the Reed country home and relayed how they had just had an automobile accident and asked if she could use the phone. Herman and Nell brought them in, fed them, and Nell loaned her car to the lady to finish getting home about a half hour down the road. Never doubting the lady would return with the car the next day, but simply showing compassion.

They were not wrong.

The next morning came with a knock at the door and a grateful young lady returning Nell's car with a beautiful bouquet of flowers. But for anyone that would try to take advantage of their kindness, Herman had no hesitancy making use of the pistol he always carried in his pickup truck. That's the way it is in the country. Herman loved to joke around and give his son-in-law and boys his daughters dated a hard time. It got to the point where he would say, "Hey, stupid, let's go for a ride," and we would all look at each other to ask which one he was talking to! Herman could let alcohol get to him, but I never saw him be mean or abusive to anyone at any time when he was drinking. He worked hard all day and didn't have a drink until all the work was done. But when he got home, he wanted his Crown Royal and a cigarette sitting at the kitchen counter.

Nell worked hard keeping the family going and feeding the farm hands. On the Reed farm, every worker got fed a hot meal at dinner time (noon), and Nell would sometimes have to take the pots of food to the field because they couldn't stop the planting or harvest to eat. Life in the Reed house meant you worked for a living and enjoyed life when you weren't working. As an old Sergeant, Herman had come home with the same determination to make things better as my father and other returning veterans had shown. Being an Air Force veteran and having grown up in a home with a disabled veteran certainly didn't make me any less in the eyes of either Nell or Herman.

While I had enjoyed hunting with Papaw's .410 shotgun for squirrels when we visited them, no one had actually taught me how to hunt. I had grown up fishing and running the river, but my treks into the mountains were more exploratory and simply enjoying nature. Herman immediately took me to his deer camp near the Morganza Spillway levees and put a rifle in my hand. When duck season opened, I was exposed to my first waterfowl hunt and immediately knew this would be my lifelong favorite. I have always enjoyed taking a deer for the venison and watching nature in the quiet forests. But hunting ducks allows me to be part of the "dance." Working hard to get that drake mallard to drop into the flooded timber always reminded me of the high school "sock hop" dances, where the girl would sheepishly try to induce the boy to cross the gym to ask her to dance. For me, pulling the trigger puts food on the table but signals the end of the real experience. It's an important part, but not the objective.

Sarah and I were married on May 22, 1976, slightly less than a year from our meeting. They tell me our reception was a really big party, but I wouldn't know because we left early to drive the seven hours to Pensacola, Florida for our honeymoon.

Dale Hall and Sarah Reed Hall, 1976

To say I didn't contribute anything to the wedding would be an understatement. I didn't even have enough money to buy Sarah an engagement ring. I swore to her that someday I would buy her a 2-carat diamond to make up for it. I took the only diamond I owned and had it fashioned into a necklace for her wedding gift. It was all I had in the world to give her at the time. Decades later, I kept my word and bought her the ring she deserved. Nell and Herman never said a word about what I or my parents should be expected to pay.

I would have never asked Momma and Leland to pay anything for my part. I was nearly 27 years old and had been on my own for almost 10 years. The thought of asking my mother for money was out of the question. Larry and Judy had eloped and simply showed up at our house in Loyall to say they were married. Momma didn't know the groom had responsibilities for the rehearsal dinner and flowers, or I know she would have offered. Sarah's Uncle Elvin stepped in and offered to have the rehearsal dinner at his home. He was an excellent cook and made wonderful gumbo and jambalaya. Until the day she died, I never told Momma about the groom's responsibilities. Sarah and I can truly say we started with nothing but her small paycheck and my GI Bill and stipend. Whatever we ended up with would be what we had earned on our own. It would have made me feel a lot better knowing Herman and Nell didn't have to carry my responsibilities for the wedding. But that's the way it was.

LSU was like a family, and several of my fellow graduate students attended the wedding. Bill Brenneman was my roommate and best man. Tim O'Brien, Frank, Ronnie, Michael Reed (Sarah's cousin), Richard, and Melvin were my groomsmen. Sarah's bridesmaids were her sisters Fernell and Phyllis, Trelle, and Sarah's good friends from Bunkie, Faye Ducote and Linda Meeker. Fred and Barbara Bryan were there to help sit on my side of the aisle. Fred got a kick out of it every time I would introduce him as my "boss" at LSU. As far as I was concerned, I got up every day and was paid to go to work. I looked at it that way and did my best to fulfill my end of the bargain.

Working in the Atchafalaya meant spending a lot of time with three good friends: Bill Brenneman, Leslie Holland, and Ed Theriot. We took samples together in Bayou Petite Prairie just outside Krotz Springs on the protected side of the levee. Bill was studying invertebrates in the sediments, Ed was studying phytoplankton, Leslie was after zooplankton, and I was collecting ichthyoplankton. Together we could demonstrate the basic food chain of plant-animal-predator and how the system fed the downstream bayous and Atchafalaya River. Mrs. Fletcher owned a small boat ramp on the banks of Bayou Petite Prairie and was like a kind grandmother to us, never charging to launch our boats or to camp overnight for our diurnal studies once she understood what we were doing. People on the Bayou are like that. They remind me a great deal of hill people in their willingness to help others.

Sarah and I were living in married student housing for $90 per month, cockroaches included at no extra cost. But we were happy in our cinderblock dwelling with two functional rooms, a cubby hole kitchen, and a bath. There was a fourth "room" that might have been big enough for a baby crib, but not a bed. We ate well because of the fish and shellfish I was able to bring home from our studies around the Basin. Each of us covered for our fellow graduate students in sample collection when conflicts arose. It was unacceptable to not stay on the rigid sampling regime, even in the face of harsh weather, sickness, or finals.

While I didn't do studies in adult fish, crawfish, shrimp, and oysters, I helped my fellow students and was able to keep our freezer with a good variety of food for a young newlywed couple to enjoy. I was happy and, regardless of the knockdowns I thought were setbacks, God had clearly been good to me. Sarah and I had been married just over a month when the United States of America celebrated its bicentennial. We were newlyweds, the greatest country on earth was 200 years old, and we were blessed to live in it.

As I started to finish up my field research (I had already completed all the coursework again for my Master's), I started looking for jobs. In those days, if you wanted a job with the federal government, you watched for the Office of Personnel Management (Op.m.) "Federal Register" to open in your professional field. Mine was Fisheries Biologist 482, and when it opened for that series in February 1977, I sent in my complete federal SF 171 job application to be classified, qualified, and be given a score at each grade. I was classified as a GS-5 with 105 points (the maximum for a veteran but not disabled veteran) and 104 at the GS-7. Once qualified, you did not apply for jobs. When a selecting official had an opening for an entry level (GS-5 or 7), they notified Op.m., and Op.m. sent them a "Certificate of Eligible Applicants" from which to choose. The official was required to start at the top of the list and make the offer. If that person declined, the official could then go to the next person on the list, and so on. Once a candidate accepted, the official was required to hire him/her. This took all bias out of hiring entry level people and made the entire country open to an applicant without the applicant having to apply multiple times. It also removed the possibility of any discrimination based on gender, race, etc. Everyone was judged solely on their credentials. I still don't understand why that approach to hiring at the entry level was later allowed to be replaced.

I also sent out over fifty applications to states, corporations, and not-for-profits looking for work. I was married and about to be finished with school and needed a J.O.B.! Only two of those companies or states had the courtesy to respond with, "We are not hiring at this time." It wasn't a good time to be looking for a job as a Fisheries Biologist in 1977. Walking by our bulletin board in the hallway that also posted job announcements, I saw an opening for a manager of a catfish farm in Yazoo City, Mississippi. Catfish farming was a new and booming industry in the fisheries community, but I was a scientist, not a farmer. While I respected farmers and how hard they worked, I expected to work in the science field answering complex questions about the ecosystem. I had learned far more than I expected about wetlands, floodplains, and how they function through my studies about fish spawning, and I wanted to pursue research positions if at all possible. But this was a job, and I needed to start getting an income.

I applied for the position with Eden Fisheries and the owner, Mr. Rodney Henderson. Mr. Henderson held an interview with me on the phone and called a day or so later to offer me the job. I would be the Farm Manager making $11,000 a year. I would have to write and defend my thesis while working full time, but I had a job! Rick Helms was the full-time mechanic, and we were the team that worked with Rodney to run the farm. When Sarah and I arrived in Yazoo City, we found a small apartment off Hwy 49E just a few miles from the farm. Sarah decided to take a few months off after our move to Mississippi, which allowed time to feel our way around in this new town and hopefully find new friends. On my first day at work, Rodney asked, "Can you weld?"

Weld? No, I am a scientist! Why would I need to know how to weld?

While I didn't say that, it's what I was thinking.

"No, sir, I can't weld."

He immediately turned to Rick and said, "Better teach him how to weld. He'll have to be helping you the same way you'll be helping him."

I learned how to weld.

I also learned how to change diesel fuel filters on tractors and well heads, replace broken water lines, paint the inside of our live haul fish truck with paint whose fumes would make you "happy" happy, and much more. I operated a backhoe, front end loader, and about everything else on the farm except the drag line excavator. That was not for amateurs. But the most important message I learned was humility. Every job on a farming operation is important, and the farm can come to a standstill based on any one of several functions. That proved true on every team I was privileged to be on. I was reminded of my upbringing and blisters digging ditches. It was a hard reminder to not leave that young boy behind and always remember to never ask someone else to do a job I had not or would not do myself. It nurtures the respect necessary to lead others.

The work was far more interesting than I had expected. Catfish prefer to spawn in holes underneath the banks of rivers, and the female stays inside the hole to protect her eggs from hungry intruders. The eggs adhere in a gelatinous mass, thus making it easy to harvest and transport them into the controlled environs of a hatchery. On the farm, old fashioned milk jugs were tied together by a long rope and stretched out along the levee to resemble holes in the bank. Fish, as with any species, will take advantage of an already existing structure instead of working to build a new one if they can. Eggs were collected from the jugs and brought into the hatchery. After the eggs hatched, efforts began immediately to start conditioning a bottom feeding fish to come to the surface and eat the formula feed that was much healthier and accelerated growth. Tapping on the side of the galvanized tanks while slowly dropping dust-like particles of feed started teaching the larvae that their food was associated with sound and was on the surface. After this conditioning, young fish less than an inch long were transferred to a fingerling pond and slowly released next to a small wooden platform.

I spent hours tapping on the side of the platform and slowly dropping food grains to lure the small fish. Once they found it, they immediately started to swarm all around the food being supplied and were ready to start receiving floating feed. It is critically important to have the natural bottom feeders come to the surface for food to see their growth, health condition, and get a feel for the numbers in the pond. While in nature, 500 pounds of fisheries biomass per acre is considered very productive for the ecosystem to support, in a farming operation we grew 10,000 pounds of fish per acre. Without the ability to observe the "crop," monitoring disease, estimating the amount of feed, and expected yield were significantly more difficult.

After working for Rodney through an entire growing season with no increase in pay and no vehicle to drive (as I had seen on other farms), he said, "Dale, you've done a good job this year and I'm grateful. Go on out there on the farm and gather yourself up 50 pounds of catfish for a Christmas bonus."

I was stunned. His farm had 400 acres of water, and I had significantly contributed to him making a profit of $1,000 per acre, much higher than any other legal agricultural crop.

"Thank you, Rodney, but you obviously need them more than I do."

It wasn't long after that I was approached by Henry Williams about hiring on with Farm Fish in Louise, Mississippi. Farm Fish had around 2,000 acres of water and was the largest catfish farm in the world. Henry offered me $13,000 a year, a new truck to drive, and the assurance that

I would never have to get in the pond again to seine fish. The last two were significant.

While doing everything on the farm, I literally got in the middle of every seining operation of the ponds using a 600-foot net pulled by two tractors, one on each levee. The seine would always capture mud from the bottom and eventually cause the bottom of the seine to bog down if the mud wasn't dumped out. That was done by workers standing in the water and one person in a small motorboat. The winter I worked for Rodney, the January cold set in and the wind blew water up on my face during the harvest operations. I had to knock the ice off my face and ears to keep from getting frostbite. I quickly grew a beard to offer a layer of insulation, and it became a permanent part of my face for the rest of my life.

What Henry was offering was no more ice forming on my face, no more dumping of mud out of the seine, and a company truck to drive. In addition, I would get paid $2,000 more per year and get a *real* Christmas bonus based on the profits of the company. Farm Fish just hired a new Farm Manager! I split the duties with another manager, with mine primarily to spawn and grow the young fish to stocking size or for sale to other farms. I had apparently established a reputation for knowing something about fisheries from growing more fingerlings for Rodney than he had ever grown and for solving a scientific mystery Rodney said would make anyone who did an instant millionaire.

Off-flavor was a real management problem for catfish farmers. When off-flavor occurred, the pond would smell like diatomaceous earth, and the fish would taste like fresh dirt. When this happened, the fish could not be sold. The pond was completely flushed with new well water while hydrated lime was applied. Eventually, the smell and taste would pass through the fish, but nothing could be done with the pond until that happened. For some farmers, that could mean the difference in being able to pay the summer bills. Only enough fish needed to pay the bills were harvested in the summer when the price was low. Most of the harvest was sold in the winter when market prices were significantly higher. When we encountered off-flavor on Rodney's farm for the first time, I asked if he would let me drive to Jackson to the nearest collegiate level library and do a little research. The symptoms gave me ideas as to where it might be coming from, but I didn't want to speculate until I could get some science behind me. He agreed, and I drove to Jackson.

It didn't take long for me to confirm my suspicions that it had to do with the rotating algal blooms in pond situations. There are many forms of algae, from single cell to filamentous, and there are different characterizations based on groupings of red, green, blue, yellow, etc. In a pond, these blooms come and go. I was looking for one with a lot of acids in their makeup that would be released when the cell died and ruptured. The usefulness of the hydrated lime indicated a base pH agent was needed to neutralize an acid, and blue-green algae fit the bill perfectly. When the bloom begins to die, the cells rupture, and multi-peptide amino acids are released in large quantities. I returned home and immediately sampled the off-flavor pond for recently ruptured and dying cells and got my confirmation of a blue-green algae die off. The answer was one of simple management to monitor the different algal blooms and plan on harvesting a pond before the blue green bloom died off and released its acids. The catfish farming world was pleased, but I didn't become a millionaire.

I had worked at Farm Fish for a full spawning, hatching, and grow out period when I got a call from the Fish and Wildlife Service. I was offered a job as a Fisheries Biologist in Vicksburg, just down the road from Yazoo City, working for the Ecological Services office there. By this time, I was confident I could return to the catfish industry if government work didn't pan out, so I said yes and quit my job with Farm Fish. In September 1978, I began my career as a federal public servant.

CHAPTER 10:

Becoming a Fed

I received the call from Joe Hardy, Field Supervisor in the Vicksburg Office, in June for my interview. He was looking to hire an entry level GS-7 biologist, and I was at the top of the Certificate of Eligible Applicants. He said he was sorry, but he could only offer me a permanent part-time position of 36 hours per week. I thought it over and told him I would accept. He got quiet on the other end of the phone, and I wondered if something was up. Joe seemed to be a true gentleman and professional in every way, so I wasn't sure if I was misreading his demeanor. He called back the next day and said he had been running the numbers and could only afford to offer me 32 hours per week. By now, the stubborn streak in me was starting to show, and I said without hesitation, "That will be fine, Joe, I'm in."

He said okay, and the paperwork was initiated. I received my official letter of hire in late August telling me to report to Vicksburg for duty on September 11, 1978. Twenty-three years later, that would become one of those dates that profoundly changed America forever. But this September 11 only changed my life.

Yazoo City is about an hour's drive north of Vicksburg, which allowed us to take our time finding a house and making the move. When I arrived at the office in the Merchant's Bank Building, I was welcomed by Joe as if there had never been any glitch in how many hours I could work. What I discovered was that Joe had a temporary employee, not to exceed six months, that he wanted to hire, but I was in the way on the Certificate. His move from full time to 36 hours to 32 hours was a ploy to get me to decline the position so he could hire Mitch King, the temporary employee who was next on the list. He hired us both at 32 hours per week, but from the very first day we were paid for 40 hours every week, worked at least 50 hours, and it was clear there was ample work for both of us. Throughout my career, it became routine to work 50-60 hours per week and only receive pay for 40. We never thought anything of it because we all did it. Over our careers, Sarah and I became close friends with Mitch and Carla King. Carla was a hairdresser and full of fun and friendliness. Their children, Dusty and Jenny, have been like family, and I know Mitch and Carla feel the same about our children. Vicksburg would not be the only time in our careers we would work together on controversial issues affecting the fish and wildlife resources.

Most of the financial support for the office came from Corps of Engineers (Corps) transfer funding to fulfill the mandate of the Fish and Wildlife Coordination Act (FWCA). That law requires the Corps to provide a FWS Report that identifies the impacts to fish and wildlife resources resulting from the project with each federal water development proposal provided to Congress. The report also identifies how much and what kind of mitigation would be necessary to offset the harmful impacts. The FWCA report was required to be attached to the Corps' Environmental Statement and General Design Memorandum provided to Congress for approval through the appropriations process.

In addition, Ecological Services was charged with the FWS responsibility to respond to Clean Water Act (CWA) Section 404 permit requests that were administered by the Corps. If a dredge or fill project occurs in Waters of the United States (WOTUS), including wetlands, the FWS role is to evaluate the proposed project, either private or governmental, and recommend issuance or denial of the permit. My introduction to the CWA and Section 404 permits was when Joe walked to my desk, handed me a copy of the law and regulations, and said, "Read these and get to know the rules of the road. You're going to be doing a lot of 404 permit work."

That was it. The full extent of my training to prepare me to represent the FWS to the Corps on permit matters. My area of responsibility included all of the Yazoo delta in Mississippi, a good portion of north Louisiana, and the entire state of Arkansas. In short order, I was the only biologist working all Clean Water Act Permits in this very large area. I was a beginning student in CWA 101, but the Avoyelles Sportsman's League lawsuit would take me from novice to journeyman in a period of months and testifying in the landmark court case that set legal definitions of WOTUS for the next 25 years. I owe Steve Forsythe and Joe Hardy a tremendous debt of gratitude for allowing me to learn and grow. Another of the important friends in my life came through my work on the Avoyelles case, also known as the Lake Ophelia Case.

Jim Tripp was the attorney representing the Environmental Defense Fund (EDF), a relatively new organization in the 1970s. Because they had little money, Jim regularly stayed with Sarah and me on his visits prior to the court hearings. A small man with wire-rimmed glasses, he lived in New York City and fit the stereotype of a New York lawyer perfectly! Jim Tripp was also one of the premier lawyers and experts on the Clean Water Act, federal water law, and the environment. To say he helped me make the transition from a biologist/naturalist to being called an expert on federal wetlands law would be an understatement. He helped me to fully understand that science is only important if it is *used* by decision-makers in setting national policy. He was the first person to make laws come alive for me and to help me understand the importance of scientifically sound data.

For the first few months, I made the hour drive each way from Yazoo City to Vicksburg in the 1967 Malibu that Momma and Leland had given me. Sarah had been working for Head Start in Yazoo City for a few months when my job offer came and remained there until we found a house in Vicksburg. It was a modest starter home at 208 High Hill Drive of about 1800 square feet, with three small bedrooms and two baths. But it was our first home, and we were happy to finally be settled. The purchase price was $38,900, which scared the hell out of me! I had never owed that much money in my life and had to adjust to the thought of a 30-year loan. Our neighbors across the street were Willis and Karoline Finch, and next door were Chester and Shirley Martin. Both couples were wonderful neighbors and friends. Willis worked on the construction of the River Bend Nuclear Plant, and Karoline was a cosmetologist. They had two small children, Jason and Shauna. Chester and Shirley moved in a year or so after we arrived and were a welcomed addition to the neighborhood. Chester was a wildlife biologist working for the Corps of Engineers at the Waterways Experiment Station. Shirly was a stay-at-home mom. They had two young children, Sharon and Jake.

Willis, Chester, and I would regularly load the back of Willis' pickup with trash on Sunday and drive to the county landfill. Sometimes we walked around looking for refuse that might have been another man's garbage, but could be our treasure. We mostly did it for grins and giggles, with beer in hand. One Sunday, I found an old TV that looked in pretty good shape, so we loaded it up and took it home. I'm not sure how sober we were, but the dump was only about a mile from our house. When I plugged it in on the carport, it had a relatively good picture, but the sound was in and out. If I could get it to work, it was better than the one we had! I had a TV repair shop give an estimate. Fifty dollars later, we had a color TV that worked just fine. Neither Willis nor Chester ever let me forget I had a "dump TV." When you start out life with nothing, a color TV that works is something.

High Hill Drive wasn't the most glamorous neighborhood in Vicksburg, but it was close to town and populated with people who were mostly in the same stage of their lives as Sarah and me. Sarah had an Oldsmobile Cutlass we had bought with money Momma shared from the proceeds of selling her house, which was used as our "family car." She found a job in Jackson teaching children with varying types of mental and physical challenges, but it required her to make the hour commute to work each day. She loved working with these children, and when I visited her at work, she had to tell me to stop treating them any differently. I wanted to hug and make them feel special, while Sarah admonished me to understand that her work was to prepare them to be like any other kid. My heart melted when I saw them, while she saw what they could be. She was gifted when it came to special needs children and continued with her daily commute up to the time when she had our first child.

We knew it was time to start having children, and Sarah became pregnant in 1979. On Wednesday morning at 7 a.m., January 9, 1980, Sarah came to me when I was getting ready for work and said, "It's time to go." She was calm; I was not. I rushed around and got the bag she had already packed for the occasion, got her in the car, and realized that I had failed the only job she had given me—to make sure the car was full of gas. Her doctor and hospital were in Jackson, only about an hour drive from Vicksburg on I-20, but I had to stop before we left town. I was a nervous wreck. Sarah was calm, other than the dead stare she was giving me as I pumped the gas.

The labor was long and difficult, but Erin Paige Hall arrived in the afternoon and captured my heart forever. Even though Erin had issues with one of her legs and neck because of her position in the womb, we were assured they were minor and could be remedied quickly. Her jet-black hair was full and the first thing we saw as she was entering this world. When I put my fingers in the crib, Erin grabbed my little finger and held on tight. I knew a joy I never thought possible. Tears flowed, and I felt a deep sense of peace. The woman I loved with all my heart had given me a beautiful daughter. I was blessed beyond compare.

Throughout and after the Lake Ophelia episode, Jim Tripp had become a close friend, not only to me but to our family. He often stayed at our home when he came down for work on Louisiana wetlands, and by the time Erin was old enough to speak, she knew the other bedroom in the house as "Mr. Jim Tripp's." One morning at breakfast, Erin asked

Jim what kind of car he drove. As a New York City dweller, Jim used mass transportation to move around the town.

"I don't own a car, Erin."

With a clearly puzzled look, she went into deep thought. Her eyes brightened. "What kind of *truck* do you drive?" When Jim answered that he didn't own a truck, Erin was stumped. How could anyone not own a car or truck?! Jim just smiled. She had no idea that her friend, Mr. Jim Tripp, would become a legend in the conservation of Louisiana wetlands.

President James (Jimmy) Earl Carter, Jr. was a peanut farmer from Plains, Georgia who had graduated from the United States Naval Academy and served in the Submarine Corp. Upon the death of his father in 1953, he resigned his commission and returned to Plains to run the family peanut business. He was an activist for civil rights in a state that staunchly resisted change, but impressed people with his down to earth approach and genuine kindness. Jimmy Carter was eventually elected Governor of Georgia and served there until his run for Presidency against Gerald Ford in 1975. Even though he was considered the underdog in the race, he won the election.

The country had not completely healed from the Watergate scandal and the resignation of President Nixon. Many were still angry at President Ford for pardoning the former President. In addition, Jimmy Carter had run on the platform that he was a Christian, the first legitimate candidate in history to use his religious beliefs in his campaign. Whatever the causes, Gerald Ford was not able to sustain the needed support to remain President. Two days after President Carter took office, he pardoned all the draft dodgers that had gone to Canada and elsewhere to avoid going into the military and the Vietnam war. It appeared he didn't comprehend the mistake of his predecessor.

On November 4, 1979, the largest single challenge to the Presidency of Jimmy Carter occurred when a group of radical students of Islam from a local Iranian college took over the Embassy in Tehran. They claimed to support the Iranian Revolution and saw the United States as an opponent of the Revolution and in support of the Shah of Iran. Shah Mohammad Reza Pahlavi had been overthrown in 1979, and the United States took him in and provided him with cancer treatments. Fifty-four Americans were held hostage under the demand that the Shah be returned to Iran for trial.

President Carter saw the act as blackmail and refused to comply with the terms of hostage release. In April 1980, he authorized "Operation Eagle Claw" to rescue the hostages. Two American warships, the USS Minitz and USS Coral Sea, which were patrolling the waters near Iran, were used as the base of operations. Helicopters deployed with special forces to carry out the rescue but were thwarted when the high sand clouds created by the helicopters began choking the engines. Eight American servicemen lost their lives in the crash of one of the helicopters. Unfortunately for President Carter, this failed rescue attempt was interpreted as a weakness in military strategy and created a significant hurdle to overcome in his bid for re-election.

In November 1979, shortly after the taking of hostages in Iran, a former Governor of California announced his intention to run for President of the United States as a Republican Party candidate. Ronald Wilson Reagan was a well-known actor and activist in the Republican party, after switching from the Democratic Party in 1963. He had unsuccessfully run for President twice before but believed there was a weakness in the Jimmy Carter presidency that he intended to use to his advantage. In addition to the questioned military strategy competence and the pardoning of draft dodgers, many saw him as naïve. In one televised debate between Carter and Reagan, Carter said he asked his young daughter Amy what she thought the most pressing issue of the world was and, "She told me nuclear proliferation."

As I watched the debate on television from a hotel room in Slidell, Louisiana, I shook my head and thought, "You're asking an eight year old for presidential advice? You're going to have a hard time in this election."

Apparently, others had a similar reaction.

The Cold War between the Soviet Union and the United States was still under way, and the chill was felt at every opportunity. The Winter Olympics were held in Lake Placid, New York that year, and tensions were high as the United States Hockey Team gradually climbed the bracket that could culminate with a U.S. versus Soviet Union game in the medal round. Criticisms were high from the United States that the Soviet athletes were not amateurs, but professionals paid to play the game for their country. The U.S. players had to find ways to support their involvement in the Olympics without being compensated, or they would be ruled ineligible.

The Soviets, as a communist/socialist government, pronounced that all people in the Soviet Union were supported by all others under a socialist system and, therefore, they were amateurs as well. On February 22, 1980, in the first game of the medal round, what would become known as the "Miracle on Ice" transpired as the U.S. beat the Soviet hockey team by a score of four to three in an astonishing display of sheer will. The Soviets were crushed. They had not only been beaten by the U.S., but by the youngest team in the Olympics. At a time when American nationalism needed a critical boost, the U.S. Olympic Hockey Team delivered. Unbeknownst at the time, this would be an omen of the demise of the Soviet Union just a few short years later.

The world was starting to change in many ways. One of the most significant occurrences of 1980 was the launch of Cable News Network (CNN), the first subscription television channel that was based on 24-hour news. Ted Turner, a multi-billionaire media developer, saw a new cable system of television with paid subscriptions offered viewers choices, but none was around the clock for breaking news at that time. He wanted to be the first. His foresight created a competitive arena for "news" that some would later curse, while others would heap adulation for its competition. Jim Lehrer, historic host of the Public Broadcasting System's News Hour, famously declared, "I am not in the entertainment business." His vision of the deterioration of "news" into sensationalism in the name of ratings was ominous. Decades later, a President of the United States would win election on the platform that anything said against him by the news media was "fake news."

Russ Earnest was a tall man of slender build and a dry wit. He was the Manager of the Jackson Area, which included Mississippi, Arkansas, Louisiana, and Alabama. Bob Misso was the Assistant Area Manager for Environment, which made the Ecological Services Field Supervisors his direct reports. Bob never gave us anything but his full support and didn't seem to care whether he had permission to take a strong position on wetland issues. If it was the right thing to do in his mind, full speed ahead. He soon developed the nicknames of "Bulldozer Bob" and "Rabid Robert." Russ was an old "fish squeezer" that had come up through the Hatchery system and had a love for the non-feathery constituents we were there to conserve.

On a visit to Greer's Ferry National Fish Hatchery, he came upon a bear of a man down in a raceway, cleaning the aftermath of a few thousand fish living there for several months; neither nice smelling nor clean duty. He said hello and got, "If you're not going to help, get the hell out of here," as a response. Russ loved this kind of no-nonsense approach to the job and appreciated David Charles Frederick and his "kill em' all and let God sort em' out" attitude. He prodded Dave to switch over to Ecological Services from Fisheries because there was more need for a combative attitude dealing with the Corps than with fishes, and Russ was leaving to go to D.C. to work in Ecological Services with Associate

Director Mike Spear. He wanted to leave the Vicksburg team as strong as possible. Dave thought about it and agreed. Dave joined the Vicksburg office in 1980, and this Marine and I immediately hit it off.

Charles Baxter had arrived as the new Field Supervisor when Joe Hardy took another position and agreed that I needed help working the 404 permits in the Yazoo Basin, Arkansas, and north Louisiana. We had gone through the ordeal of the Lake Ophelia case and had developed the new "Multiple Parameter Approach to Jurisdictional Wetland Determination," the common name for Waters of the U.S. under the Clean Water Act. (A full discussion of the Lake Ophelia Case can be found in my book, COMPELLED.)

Through that case, I became known as one of the experts in this new methodology. He assigned Dave to work with me. I, in turn, was to teach Dave about the jurisdictional wetlands' turnaround. In the flurry of permit requests following the court case, I had been overwhelmed and only able to respond to bottomland hardwood wetland permits at the *10,000-acre level and above*. Together, we were to stop all bottomland hardwood wetland losses. No problem.

CHAPTER 11:

Clear Lake

One of the shocks of having a new baby was the loss of Sarah's income. Sarah rightfully took time off to be with our new daughter and to make sure she fully recovered from the neck and leg injuries at birth, and only returned to work half time until we made our next duty station move. Sarah had to push Erin's head from side to side to force the muscles on the weak side of her neck to work and grow. I helped out some, but it was mostly Sarah because it tore me apart to hear Erin cry and know I was the cause. But it had to be done daily so her neck would develop properly. It worked well and, by her second birthday in 1982, she was fully healed. Shirley Martin helped by babysitting Erin when Sarah was at work, but the reduction in spendable income was dramatic.

When Erin was born, I was a GS-9, and suddenly our income went from two people with two incomes to three people with one income. During the time before Sarah returned to work half time, my "allowance" was $5/week. That was to buy gas and any beer I could find cheap enough. Shirley Martin had found beer in white cans that only said "BEER," no brand name, for 99 cents a six pack. I was in! Through carpooling, cheap beer, and the time I was on the road for work, we made it through until Sarah was able to go back to work half-time at Family Development in Vicksburg. But with the realization that my income was going to be our permanent primary source, I knew I needed to get promotions as quickly as I could to raise my salary. I was promoted to a GS-11 in 1980, and that helped us begin the process of getting back on our feet. As 1982 got under way, Sarah and I were beginning to come out of the deep financial strain we had been feeling, and I started putting out job applications to other FWS offices. As much as I loved what I was doing, I needed to find ways to be promoted. Erin was becoming quite the little princess. She loved to walk around on her tiptoes, ride the three-wheeler with Dad, and give great hugs. We knew if we were going to move again, it would be much better before she started kindergarten.

A job opening showed up on the "green sheets," so called because the pages were green to be easily identified as job announcements within the FWS. I was a GS-11 and at the maximum grade for my staff position. While Charles and Bob Misso openly tried to get me to stay longer, they couldn't offer me a GS-12 position and understood when I applied for the job of Outer Continental Shelf Coordinator for the Western Gulf of Mexico. The position was housed in Galveston, Texas, and the office was supervised by Floyd Nudi. There were only two such positions in the Gulf of Mexico, one for the Eastern Gulf and one for the Western. The role of that position was to protect sensitive shorelines and submerged ecosystems, such as coral reefs, by placing lease stipulations on oil and gas operations in the Gulf that were overseen by the Department of the Interior. The leases were administered by the Minerals Management Service, but required FWS stipulations be included on any leases offered for bid.

Floyd knew of my work in bottomland hardwood wetlands in the Lower Mississippi Valley and offered me the job of OCS Coordinator for the Western Gulf. The only protected area offshore in the Western Gulf is a salt dome coral reef called the Flower Gardens, directly off the Texas coast. Floyd later admitted that he knew the OCS job would be minimally challenging and planned to make use of my wetlands experience in other areas of office responsibility. In what would become a normal course of business, I had to leave Sarah and Erin behind in Vicksburg until our house sold and they could join me in Texas. Almost as soon as I arrived, Floyd moved the office from Galveston to Clear Lake, near the NASA Headquarters. While the new position was a GS-12 with a fair increase in pay, we still could not afford the expenses of two places to live.

I found a bedroom with bath for rent in a house trailer that was owned by a single man in his 40s. Alan Kingsbury was a kind and gentle soul who had two small dogs and was a dispatcher for the local police department. My assumption that he was gay was confirmed when he brought "friends" home to spend the night with him. I had no issue with his sexual orientation but was concerned that my food in the refrigerator be left alone by his guests, and no one was to come into my bedroom or bathroom for *any* reason. He assured me that would be the case and, between his night work schedule and my day work schedule, we seldom saw each other. He was a good man, and it worked out for both of us. There was simply no way I could afford even a studio apartment in addition to our mortgage note, so I was happy to have a place to sleep for only $50 a week.

Until Sarah and Erin could join me, we tried to see each other at least every two weeks when she would drive to Bunkie from Vicksburg, and I would drive from Houston. It was about a four-hour drive for each of us and less than ideal when my wife and two-year-old daughter were an eight-hour drive away. Floyd and his wonderful wife Pat were like second parents to me and did all they could to ease the strangeness of living in "the home," as the trailer came to be known. Their son, Mark, and daughter, Michelle, were wonderful kids and treated me like an uncle. I had more new friends for life. I found that to be a constant in the world of conservation. Everyone who engages in conservation is committed to helping and giving back. Everyone is family.

Sarah and Erin joined me six months later, and we found a home in Seabrook, about a ten-minute drive from work. We had wonderful neighbors next door in Dave and Lex Barker. Behind us were Barry and

Kathy Dubbin, and just down the street were Larry and Rose Leewright. They were all great friends and helped look after Sarah during the many absences when I was travelling for work. By then, Floyd had accepted a job in Albuquerque and was in preparation to move. Bruce Halstead was the Assistant Field Supervisor and hated Houston almost as much as Floyd and Pat. They were all from the west and found the heat, humidity, and traffic unbearable. In short order, Bruce also took a job as Field Supervisor in the Albuquerque Field Office and moved in the summer of 1983.

Mike Spear had moved from his Associate Director position in Washington to be the Regional Director of the Southwest Region, which included Texas. He had been most adamant that one needed Washington Office experience in order to become a Field Supervisor but knew me from the Lake Ophelia case and very much wanted me to replace Floyd. Under the promise that I would move to D.C. for national office experience after Clear Lake, Mike was able to convince Director Bob Jantzen to allow me to be promoted to Field Supervisor, GS-13. Between going from a GS-11 to a GS-13 in two years, and finally selling our house in Vicksburg, we were back together once again and starting to have a little less stress on the budget. With Sarah's desire to be a full-time mom, we switched to the mindset that we would make all economic decisions based on whatever salary I was making. By coming to that conclusion, we found our family options increased by removing her job needs from consideration.

Some amazing things were happening in the United States in 1982. On March 26, ground was broken on the Washington Mall to build a monument to the Vietnam War and all who lost their lives. It would be a place of reflection and prayer, honoring those who gave all. The nation needed healing, and many who cursed us when we were in uniform now wanted to honor those who died. It was good for America. But for those of us who served, either in Vietnam or in support of our nation in other parts of the world, there was never a "Welcome Home." Only those who served during those times can appreciate the hurt we felt being called fascist baby killers and being spit at simply because we were in the uniform of our country. But we were, and still are, grateful for the recognition of those whose check was cashed by the American people. Their blood bought our freedom, and those who proudly wear the uniform today continue to pay the price. I will always love and honor my brothers and sisters in arms.

In December, two historic events occurred. TIME Magazine recognized the Personal Computer as its "Man of the Year." In making the announcement, TIME released a statement that read, in part, "In the fairly near future, home computers will be as commonplace as television sets or dishwashers. There are some occasions, though, when the most significant force in a year's news is not a single individual but a process, and a widespread recognition by a whole society that this process is changing the course of all other processes. That is why, after weighing the ebb and flow of events around the world, TIME has decided that 1982 is the year of the computer."

We didn't have computers in our Fish and Wildlife Service offices because there was no budget to buy them, but we knew things were changing. When we finally got a computer in Clear Lake, it was only to be used to log wetland permits. Our reports were still written on yellow legal pad paper, handed to a typist, and prepared in that manner. Times were changing, but the government was still the government. The most significant advancement in science, however, was the first artificial heart implant that wasn't immediately rejected by the host. One had been attempted in 1969, but the patient's body rejected it almost immediately. Dr. Robert Jarvik, a Medical School graduate at the University of Utah that went into research instead of medical practice, developed what was known as Jarvik 7 and placed it in the chest of a Seattle area retired dentist.

Dr. Barry Clark received his mechanical heart on December 2, 1982, and lived for another 112 days with his body being supplied blood by an artificial pump. This single accomplishment in medicine made me stop and reflect on the Army doctors that had to tell my father they couldn't remove the shrapnel because it was too close to his heart and, because of that, he would have only 20 years to live. To think that medicine had advanced from the point of not being able to open a patient's chest and operate, to being able to completely remove the heart and replace it with an artificial pump that worked for nearly four months, was beyond remarkable. But that would prove to be only the beginning of heart disease treatment, transplants, and amazing growth in medical knowledge.

Sarah quickly adapted to being the stay-at-home mom and was always there for Erin as I continued to have travel requirements. Erin quickly developed into the beautiful young Brownie, ballerina, and all-around gymnast. She was her dad's "Big Girl" and remained so, even into adulthood. I accept my bias, but Erin was a beautiful girl with long black hair and her mother's physique. Still regularly walking on her toes, she became infatuated with Mary Lou Retton. In the course of my regular travels, I encountered Ms. Retton in an airport while we were both waiting for a connection flight. I asked her to give her autograph for my daughter and was surprised that she seemed irritated. She gave it "To Erin," and I walked away thinking less of this person who desperately wanted the recognition and money, but felt it an inconvenience to give her autograph to a four-year-old girl who idolized her. Nevertheless, Erin was thrilled. While I had to travel regularly for work, Sarah was always there to see that Erin was in Brownies, ballet, and all other activities that were so important at that time in her life.

Dave Frederick contacted me after I took over as Field Supervisor asking for help in getting him out of Vicksburg. He believed Charles Baxter was "out to get him" and asked if I could bring him over to Clear Lake with me. I wasn't surprised that Dave and Charles may have had conflicts. They could not have been more opposite in personalities. Charles was an expert on the Corps' planning process for water development projects but also carried a book under his arm on "how to be a supervisor." He needed it. I thought the world of Charles, but he was not cut out to be a supervisor and handle the personnel issues that come with it. To his credit, he eventually volunteered to transfer to the supervisor position in a planning office where supervision was a minor duty, and he again excelled. I had plans for Dave to join me long before he called, but I couldn't share those with him.

He knew the Senior Staff Biologist position I had moved into from my OCS position was now open and asked if I would be willing to let him have the job. I had been Dave's friend and mentor while I was at Vicksburg and made sure he received credit for the work he did in helping me, but I understood his rugged Marine approach to things rubbed other people wrong. The Senior Field biologist is the first stop for a staff biologist looking for advice, scientific guidance or counsel. Dave was a "get it done" kind of person, but I didn't believe he was the right person for the senior staff job. I knew he was hurting and wanted badly to get out of Vicksburg, but I had to tell my friend no. "Dave, you'll just have to trust me. You're not the right person for that job." My professional ethics wouldn't allow me to give him the job over another biologist in the office, Allan Mueller, whom I felt was better qualified and better suited. I could hear the agony over the phone as he said, "Okay, I trust you."

Within six months, I was officially promoted to the position of Field Supervisor and placed my now vacant Assistant Field Supervisor position out for competition. I called Dave and asked, "Are you ready to come join me now? The job of Assistant Field Supervisor is open, and you're the one I want for my number two. Get your application in."

"You bet your ass! It will be in tomorrow!" he said.

I told him to take his time and make sure the application reflected all his background in leading others, especially in the Marine Corps. He did his part, and in May 1984, Dave reported to Clear Lake as our new Assistant Field Supervisor. I turned over most of the day-to-day operations to Dave and worked on building relationships with the Colonel at the Corps, the state Parks and Wildlife Director, and others. I became the face of the office to the public, and Dave became the train engineer. With Allan as Senior Staff and Dave as my Assistant, I had the team that I knew would get the job done.

One of the critical lessons we learned when Sarah decided she wanted to be a stay-at-home mom was if you wait until you think you can afford a child, you'll never have one. Somehow, you find a way to support the family you love and simply forget about the things you can't afford. We decided it was time for a second child and were blessed with a son on July 7, 1984. Adam Nicholas Hall was born a little after 8 a.m., and this time I was ready to cut the umbilical cord. Sarah and I had both forgotten the privilege that is extended to the father when Erin was born but made sure to remember for Adam. I experienced that indescribable feeling of fatherhood once again. I now had a son to go with our beautiful Erin, and I could not have felt more blessed. His hair was as black as Erin's, and his hand around my finger had the repeated effect. Tears flowed.

We had a sad time in November 1985, when we lost our beloved Callie Colwell to throat cancer. All those years of rolling her own cigarettes, dipping the very strong snuff, and receiving little medical care resulted in losing the struggle with cancer. We were pleased she was able to see her great-grandson, Adam, but she unfortunately never lived to see her wonderful Emily. Sarah and I got the news that she was in the hospital and would likely not recover, so we were blessed to be there with

Papaw and several aunts and uncles when she passed. She was the true matriarch of the Colwell family. I still miss her today.

Erin was becoming quite the ballerina and loved being a Brownie scout. She naturally walked on her tip toes, so ballet was a perfect fit. Slender and agile, her father's heart melted every time I saw her dance. She was sweet, kind to other children, and loved having her best friend, Lindsay, come visit. Sarah brought in a little extra income babysitting Lindsay during the school year. Adam was immediately into everything! Almost as soon as he could walk, we were having to pay extra attention to where he was and what he was doing. It seemed he wasn't satisfied with walking and getting into things at ground level. He also loved to climb!

I once walked into our cubby hole of a kitchen and found Adam sitting on top of the microwave on the counter! He had climbed up the door facing and got on the microwave. He was smiling as if to say, "I knew I could do it!" Thankfully, one of the blessings of having a climber is they seem to be more attentive to how they climb. Each climb is carefully thought out. He had very few falls. Adam was energy in motion! Sarah's brother, Melvin, referred to him as "Adam's Pest Control" because he was always into everything. Barry and Kathy Dubbin were wonderful neighbors, and Barry became one of my best friends. He worked at a factory that made pipeline gaskets of stainless steel. When I wasn't travelling, Barry and I had beers either in our backyards connected by a fence gate or in our living rooms. He would eventually help me bring the Clear Lake office together as a team.

Floyd had inherited an office that was in shambles. The former supervisor was said to have smoked marijuana in the office, and it was in the federal courthouse at the time! He was also accused of shouting profanities down the hall at his employees and keeping records to see if he could fire them ... any of them. I was able to confirm the record keeping when I became Field Supervisor. I found separate personnel files in the file cabinet on each staff member. There were notes in each documenting what he believed were improper actions by the employee.

I personally carried each one down to the dumpster and threw them away. But I had a morale problem to deal with. In addition to Dave, I also brought that sweet young lady with a bucket full of talent, Elaine Smith, to Clear Lake and gave her a chance to show what she could do in the field of administration. She had been a clerk typist in Vicksburg, and a very good one. I watched as we provided our hand-written reports on yellow legal paper to be typed in draft, then again after our edits and on to making multiple copies using carbon paper. Most employees today have no idea what it was like writing reports and communications back then. One of the most amazing days for office clerks was when our offices got their first magnetic card machines. The typist could actually type into a machine, have a mag card record all the input, then simply make the changes to the mag card for a final document! Then, all they had to do was punch a key, and the machine typed out the entire document. They were dancing in the aisles!

I knew Elaine had the talent. She simply lacked the self-confidence. When she came to Texas, she had just met the man of her dreams, and they decided to get married. Lucien Schaffer was an upstart engineer, and they made a wonderful couple. Because she and Lucien were both living in Texas, and her father had passed away, she asked if they could be married in our home. We were delighted! In addition, she asked if I would walk her down the aisle. It is one of the true honors of my life. In Sarah's and my living room, I was able to answer the question, "Who brings this bride to be married?" with, "Her Mother and I do."

Elaine, Lucien, Lauren, and Daniel are as much a part of our family as any relative could be. Sarah and I are proud to have been able to be part of their lives. Elaine went on to retire as a GS-12 in Administration, a high achievement for someone without a college degree.

I wanted to try and bring the Clear Lake team together on a social level and needed Dave and Elaine's help to do so. A crawfish boil is a social event, not just a meal. I believed if we could bring the staff and their counterparts in the Corps, National Marine Fisheries Service, and state fish and wildlife agencies together on a social level, we could continue to rebuild the trust Floyd had begun. My good friend Barry provided a well needed piece of the puzzle. To boil an entire 40-pound sack of crawfish at once, one needs a *large* pot. When I asked Barry if his guys at the plant could make one with the stainless steel they used to make pipeline gaskets, he grinned that big Barry grin and said, "Does a duck like water?"

They built a pot that, to my knowledge, is still in use at Clear Lake's annual crawfish boils, now over four decades old. Fred Werner, Brian Cain, Allan Mueller, Carlos Mendoza, B.D. King, Julie Massey, Denise Baker, Dawn Whitehead, and the entire crew grew into a true FWS family. The boil was the beginning. Dave and Joyce accepted the role of surrogate parents to the young folks and parties at homes of staff became a regular occurrence. Trust returned and led to one of the best teams in which I have ever been honored to belong.

The largest Corps of Engineers water development project within our responsibility was the Galveston Bay Area Navigation Study, also known as the Houston Ship Channel project. Houston was a 40-foot port, meaning it could handle only cargo ships that could navigate in 40 feet or less of channel. The Port of Houston wanted desperately to increase the depth of the channel going the entire length of Galveston Bay to 50 feet. This was no small undertaking and would move millions of cubic yards of dredged material throughout the bay. We assigned Fred Werner, one of our seasoned biologists, to lead the effort. While Fred was a character and quite the handful, there was no question about his capability to lead the team. As part of my efforts to be the face of the office, I struck up a relationship with Harold Scarlett, the environmental writer for the Houston Post. I learned through the Lake Ophelia effort that biologists were terrible about getting in front of the public and providing the information needed to support any given effort. Biologists seemed to think, "Just trust me, I'm your representative on science," but real strength in conservation is found in eliminating public ignorance and replacing it with facts and knowledge. It is another form of respect when the power of information is shared. I was determined to have the people of Houston understand what these projects meant to them and their quality of life. I was, however, also determined to leave the biologists alone to do their work and accept the new responsibilities I had as their supervisor. I had learned that one of the worst forms of supervision is to want the pay and recognition as a supervisor, but still try to do the work of the biologist. It doesn't work.

Through the different issues, Harold Scarlett had learned to trust what I told him because I never told him anything I couldn't prove, or believed to be true, and I made sure he knew the difference. There is no greater asset a news reporter can have than a source that can be consistently trusted. Trust drives all relationships, be they in love, friendship, or business. We believed the Galveston Bay project would have been disastrous. One of the main issues we had not been equipped to handle in the past, but now could, was that of environmental contaminants.

The FWS had created the Environmental Contaminants Program at the urging of and support from Congressman Sidney Yates. Dr. Brian Cain joined our office about the same time I came over from Vicksburg. He had been a professor at Texas A&M and was extremely capable in the field of toxicology. Through his knowledge of how dangerous chemicals are "sealed" over time into the layers of sediment beneath the bay bottom, we were able to do core samples and identify the exact chemicals that would be released by a dredge cutting ten feet deeper, and in what concentrations. In addition, bays are the confluence of freshwater flows and ocean salt water to create the highly productive estuary, where salinity gradients go from near zero to 35 parts per thousand of pure sea water just outside the mouth of the bay.

Jim Blackburn was an attorney and law professor at Rice University who joined with the state and our team to fight the project. Jim Bob, as I affectionately called him in reference to his roots in Texas, is one of the most accomplished environmental attorneys I was privileged to meet in my career. His dedication to conservation of the Texas coast, and particularly Galveston Bay, was unmatched. This was his home, and he was committed to seeing it conserved. Harold Scarlett did his job and regularly ran articles giving Houstonians factual information about how the Corps didn't seem committed to a proper analysis, either of environmental impacts or potential alternatives. This was truly a paradigm change for the city of Houston, state of Texas, and the Texas Parks and Wildlife Commission.

Our FWCA Report stated that there were unacceptable environmental damages that would occur as a result of the project. If these problems were not addressed and remedied, the report said, the FWS would elevate this project to the President's Council on Environmental Quality for resolution of issues. The public depended on the scientists in government to let them know when there were potentially harmful effects and when there weren't. We took that responsibility seriously. The 50-foot channel was never approved, partly because of the professional work done by a dedicated field staff in Clear Lake with our state and public partners, and partly because the move towards super tankers subsided, thus reducing the need for a deeper channel. Regardless of the actual reasons, it was our job to make sure all concerns were honestly and properly addressed *before* the project moved forward to the point of irretrievable impacts. Many complain about the slow pace of government decision-making. The Galveston Bay Area Navigation Study proved to be an excellent example of why major government actions should not be rushed to judgement.

On Tuesday, January 28, 1986, I was sitting at my desk and Frances Garza, one of our clerks, walked into my office with a stunned look on her face.

"The Challenger shuttle just blew up." It was about 10:40 a.m. central time. We had neither TVs nor computers in the office, so we turned on the radio. The office was in shock, as was the rest of the world. These were not just astronauts; these were neighbors. I called one of my friends that worked at NASA and offered any assistance we could give to the families and co-workers, knowing there really was nothing we could do. But this was our government family. It was a cold morning in Florida with temperatures dipping below freezing. The flight engineers were concerned about the performance of seals on the solid rocket boosters based on past performance, but the decision was made by flight command to proceed with the launch.

Later investigations revealed poor communication within the flight command network that contributed to the suppression of this critical information. The engineers were, unfortunately, correct. The crew of the STS-51L mission was composed of NASA Astronauts Gregory Jarvis, Judy Resnik, Dick Scobee, Ronald McNair, Michael Smith, Ellison Onizuka, and Teacher In Space participant Christa McAuliffe. The seals had failed to perform in the past, and when records were researched, it was discovered they had significant failure in freezing temperatures. Salvage crews spent several weeks recovering pieces of the shuttle and carefully bringing up the remains of the astronauts. The final resting place for those unidentified was a Monument to the Challenger Crew, Arlington National Cemetery, dedicated May 20, 1986. It was a hard day for America. While we value adventure and progress, we value life more.

In the spring of 1986, I was contacted by Bob Jacobson, Assistant Regional Director for Ecological Services in Alaska, to ask if I would be willing to come to Alaska and temporarily run the ES office in Fairbanks while they recruited a new supervisor. I had two questions: From when to when? Will I be able to maintain the full per diem rate for the whole time?

The timeframe was from breakup to freeze-up, or for the summer months. That was important because I was not interested in leaving my wife and two children for four months, given the amount of time we had spent apart during the move. The second question about per diem was related to the same. I wanted my family to accompany me and, to have an apartment large enough for us, I would need the full per diem rate to continue throughout our stay instead of being reduced after each thirty days. That, too, was approved.

I went ahead of Sarah, Erin, and Adam and found a place in Fairbanks in preparation for their arrival when school let out for the summer. It was one of the most enjoyable times of our lives, especially watching our children see and experience new surroundings. One of those was 24 hours of light each day. On one occasion, there was a knock at our apartment door around 1 a.m. When Sarah and I both got out of bed to open the door, we saw the sweet little girl that lived upstairs asking, "Can Erin come out and play?" We had maintained our normal schedule for bedtime to avoid serious adjustments when we returned home and had to tell the little girl Erin was in bed. Her response was one of incomprehension. We learned that the parents of children in Alaska had to deal with keeping their children happy and safe during the terrible winter months with temperatures as low as -40 degrees Fahrenheit, so when summer arrived, they let their children restore the strength of their muscles by playing until they literally fell asleep. We never questioned the legitimacy of that approach.

During our stay, Herman, Nell, and Phyllis used Phyllis' ability to have her parents and herself fly free and came to visit. It was a wonderful time. I took Herman fishing down at Homer and, during the lengthy drive down through Denali National Park and all the beauty we passed, I found Herman continually fighting his body wanting him to fall asleep. When I told him to go ahead and take a nap, he said, "Sheet, I'm afraid

I'll miss somethin'!" That was Herman. He had told me he wanted to go salmon fishing while he was there.

I said, "Herman, I don't think you want to do that. Let's go halibut fishing instead."

He asked why and I said, "In Alaska, at the height of the salmon runs, it is often referred to as 'combat fishing.'" When we passed through Anchorage on our way to Homer to go halibut fishing, Herman looked out his window as we crossed the bridges and understood. The fishermen were literally lining the riverbanks within two feet of each other. He said, "I think I'll like halibut fishing better."

It was a wonderful summer, and we created memories we will always cherish.

By 1987, I was starting to feel as if we were re-visiting conservation issues we had addressed five years earlier, and we already knew the correct way to approach them. It was either time to move to the next job or accept that life would simply not be as challenging as I needed it to be. I never forgot my promise to move to D.C., so I began applying for positions there. One of those was the Deputy Assistant Director-Fisheries, a GS-14/15 position. Gary Edwards was the Assistant Director-Fisheries and had come in with Bob Jantzen at a career SES position. While not a career FWS employee, he was a good person and was eventually accepted by the FWS Fisheries family. I didn't believe I had very much chance for success, but I was a fisheries biologist and willing to work in other Programs of the FWS. I wanted the powers that be to understand my commitment to the TEa.m.. To my surprise, I got the job. In late 1987, I loaded my 1976 Ford F150 and headed to D.C., again without Sarah, Erin, and Adam.

CHAPTER 12:

Life in Virginia

Gary Edwards proved to be a good man with a kind heart. Bob Jantzen had been the Director of the Arizona Game and Fish Department, and Gary was a Regional Supervisor under Bob. When Bob was made Director, he brought Gary in with him and gave him the grade of Senior Executive Service (SES). That didn't sit well with the career rank and file of the FWS. The SES positions are highly coveted, and most employees spend their entire careers never getting close. At the time, the maximum grade for a FWS Hatchery Manager was GS-12, and most were GS-11.

But Gary won everyone over with his willingness to admit what he didn't know and to depend on the seasoned Fisheries staff to guide him. Gary shared with me that I got the position because he couldn't convince any of the Fisheries Assistant Regional Directors or their Deputies to take the job and decided he would make a point by hiring someone from outside the Program. I benefitted because I was willing to do what the agency needed me to do and go where they needed me to go. I have little sympathy for people that believe they should be able to sit in one spot and be promoted with only limited geographic experience. With tears in my eyes as I again said goodbye to Sarah and my two children, I made the trip to D.C. and temporary housing in November 1987.

Texas was an oil-based economy, and Houston was at the epicenter of the petroleum industry. No one could have ever predicted that oil would hit rock bottom and the industry would hand out pink slips on a Thursday telling thousands of employees they were being laid off on Friday. Governor Mark White was infuriated and vowed that Texas would never be solely dependent on the petroleum industry again. He went to work recruiting a diversity of industries to Texas. But for Sarah and me, it was of little help. Our house was on the market in Harris County along with hundreds of others belonging to laid off oil patch workers, and there were hardly any buyers. Because we had made no money on our house in Vicksburg, I had taken advantage of being a veteran and obtained a GI loan with no down payment. We had a house with the full mortgage, no buyers, and I was in D.C. without my family. After giving it about six months of no offers, we finally accepted an offer from another veteran to simply take over the GI loan. In addition, we had put solar panels on the roof and owed several thousand dollars on that. At closing, we as sellers had to write a check for $4,000. But we were free of debt in Houston, and my family could join me.

Since my original GI loan had been assumed under the qualifications of another veteran, my eligibility was restored, and we took out another GI loan for a house in Hamilton, Virginia, just north of Leesburg. The sticker price was shocking! We left a home in Houston with a $600 per month note to buy a house in Virginia with a $1,500 per month mortgage! Because we had to buy far from D.C. to afford the house we bought, I would have at least an hour's commute to work each day. But we were together and had a small home in a community we truly loved. Northern Virginia is highly agriculture with equestrian farms all around. Our home was in Hamilton, about halfway between Leesburg and Purcellville. On weekends, we often saw the fox and hound hunters ride by in their red outfits. The kids and Sarah loved it there, as did I. Unfortunately, I had to deal with the energy-draining commute each day, but being that far out of town was the best we could afford.

Times were very tough financially, but my family and I were keeping our promise to the agency and gaining new experience to hopefully take to my next assignment. Over time, however, it took its toll on both Sarah and me. Sarah was now in a town with few friends and no relatives within hundreds of miles, two young children, and a household to keep up, and I had nearly no home time. As the number two fisheries officer of the FWS, I now had responsibility to support activities all over the country. Between my draining 12-14-hour days and geographically broader travel, it started to test the strength of our marriage. It's easy to start thinking one's partner had it easier than you, and that began to creep in on both of us. Thankfully, we found a way to work through it. Giving up was not an option. But to say the financial stresses and challenging work schedule brought stress into our home and marriage would be an understatement.

Ronald Reagan had completed his two terms as President, and George H. W. Bush, his Vice President, was elected in November of 1988. The most prominent occurrence during the Reagan terms, other than the assassination attempt on his life and the largest tax hike in history, was the beginning of the fall of the Soviet Union. The collapse didn't occur until 1991. But many believe his influence on Gorbachev was highly relevant. Most believe it was due to the liquidation of gold assets by the Soviet Union to keep pace with the Cold War and the Space Race. They were on a clear path of bankruptcy. The leader of the Soviet Union, Mikhail Gorbachev, knew they could not continue down this path and introduced two major programs that led to the eventual breakup of the USSR, Glasnost, and Perestroika.

Glasnost, or political openness, eliminated many of the iron hand programs that were the hallmark of the Communist form of government. Through Glasnost, Gorbachev allowed newspapers and journalists to criticize the government, he released many political prisoners and eliminated much of the secret police. In the throngs of economic collapse,

Perestroika allowed free market ownership of businesses by individuals and cooperatives, allowed workers to strike for better conditions and wages, and encouraged foreign investment. Unfortunately for Mr. Gorbachev, these changes were too little and much too late. The economy could simply not rebound fast enough, and the individual Soviet states became emboldened and were declaring independence.

The entire eastern block of Europe, including East Germany, became free states. On Christmas Day, 1991, the flag of the Soviet Union flew over the Kremlin in Moscow for the last time. While many in the know credit the stealth work of the 6917th Security Group in San Vito, Italy during the late 1960s and early 1970s for laying the groundwork for the fall of the Soviet Union, those of us who were involved are too modest to comment.

Erin loved her school, and Adam was preparing for pre-school with a tank full of energy! Erin and Adam loved each other very much, and it warmed my heart to see how Erin included Adam in her "game show" and "hotel owner" skits with her friends. We were able to get some on film, and I hope they find time to enjoy them with their children. I tried all the different possibilities for the commute to the Interior Building at 1849 C St, NW: local Amtrack train, bus, carpool, and driving. About my second year on the job, Frank Dunkle, the new FWS Director, rented a building in Arlington, Virginia for our staff, and I was offered an office there instead of the Main Interior Building Downtown. In addition, because I was the Deputy Assistant Director, I was given a parking space in the building at no cost! I bought a new 1989 Nissan Hardbody pickup that got much better gas mileage than the old F150, and the decision on how to commute became simple. I drove. While taking on a new truck payment was not our first choice, I used to say, "The F150 will pass up anything on the highway except a gas station."

In 1988, Sarah and I received some surprising news. We were once again going to be parents! Our surprise child was born on December 29. Emily Claire Hall came into the world seeing her father cry just as I had for the first two. While Sarah and I had worried how we could afford another child, any worries completely disappeared when I cut my daughter's umbilical cord and held Emily for the first time. The love of a parent is so powerful all other issues or worries disappear when one's child takes her/his first breath. There is simply no description that adequately portrays the emotional volcano that springs forth with the birth of a child. From the first moments, I have thanked God for knowing we needed Emily in our lives. Sarah always had an outgoing personality and quickly got into the local community atmosphere and the small schools the children attended. She settled in as the homemaker and classroom mom. One of the wonderful experiences I was able to share with Sarah and our children was when scientists from the Soviet Union visited.

The FWS and its equivalent in the Soviet Union had signed a protocol of exchange, much like the one I worked on with the Chinese. One of the things they were interested in was how we handled the myriad of "low head hydropower" dams sprinkled across the northeast U.S. Low head hydro dams were simply weirs or dams that were much smaller than western U.S. dams and are found scattered across New England. Gary asked me to lead the tour of the group across the northeastern states and generally be their host. Two things that struck me about their culture while we were touring was their eating and drinking habits. They were provided the normal U.S. per diem allowance for food, which usually was $33/day, depending on location. I noticed the Soviet scientists wanted to stop at markets each day so they could buy bread and meat for sandwiches. They each chipped in so they would have the most they could to spend on electronics.

Apparently in the Soviet Union, the latest in electronic products were very hard to find. In addition, they always bought a fresh bottle of American whiskey, from bourbon to gin. In the evening when they opened the bottle, they threw away the lid! I learned that they expected to drink the entire bottle and, hopefully, get drunk. I came to learn it was a form of despair and a loss of hope. One of the stops occurred on my birthday, and I decided to join them in their nightly ritual. I bought a bottle of tequila since they had not tried that on the trip, and they immediately formed a liking to it. I told them it came from cacti and agave plants in the southwest and Mexico. The next morning, they declared with great headaches that tequila was the "drink with many spines." I had to agree.

When we returned to D.C., I invited them to come to our home and have a homemade American dinner. They loved the idea, and Erin was allowed to invite her best friend and their parents. The scientists could not have been more gracious nor kind. They enjoyed every minute of the visit but were surprised that I was performing an upgrade of our basement myself. They assumed I "hired others" to do all the work around my home since I was a high-level government official. I had to break the news to them that, while I was a high-level official of the U.S. government, we didn't get paid as much as they thought. Before the evening ended, one of the scientists took Erin's colored pencils and drew her a picture of what he saw outside his window near a lake outside Moscow. When she brought it to me in the other room, I told her to go tell him, "Spasiba," which is "thank you" in Russian. When she did, a large grin immediately appeared, and he gave her a big hug. Sometimes I wonder if we shouldn't let the children of the world lead our diplomacy.

In late 1990, President Bush ordered American troops, ships, and aircraft to Saudi Arabia as a staging point to protect Kuwait against the invasion of Iraq and Saddam Hussein. Previously backed by the U.S. in the Iraq-Iran War, Hussein was beginning a significant effort to retake Kuwait, a part of Iraq in times of the Ottoman Empire. The U.S. saw Iraq as a supporter of Terrorists, but apparently wanted to see Iran defeated more than they wanted Iraq controlled. Iraq also believed Kuwait was exceeding oil production quotas established by the Organization of the Petroleum Exporting Countries (OPEC) in the Middle East. The U.S.

downplayed the Iraq threats to invade Kuwait and reclaim both their previous territory and the oil reserves it held, but in July 1990, Iraq positioned 30,000 troops on the Iraq-Kuwait border, triggering the placement of the U.S. Fleet in the Persian Gulf on full alert.

Hussein had made it clear to the Arab League that he believed Iraq was owed $10 billion for the illegal withdrawal of oil from the Rumaila oil field. The U.S. Ambassador to Iraq, April Glaspie, met with Hussein in Bagdad to try and calm the rhetoric. But those efforts failed. The U.S. had historically taken a neutral position on disputes between Arab countries, but rich oil fields were at stake and Iraq was threatening the safety of Saudi Arabia, a U.S. ally. Kuwait offered $500 million to Iraq as reparation for extracted oil, which triggered an immediate Iraq invasion on August 2, 1990.

The ship and troop buildup ordered by President Bush was in response to Britain Prime Minister Margaret Thatcher's concerns about the invasion. The UN Security Council placed immediate economic sanctions against Iraq, and a coalition of 35 countries committed to the protection of Kuwait and its neighbors. The buildup was completed by the end of the year, and on January 17, 1991, a war was waged by the coalition forces codenamed "Operation Desert Storm." The forces were led by General "Stormin" Norman Schwarzkopf, Jr., and constituted the single largest coalition since World War II.

By February, the massive aerial assault had crippled all Iraqi military forces, and on February 24, ground troops entered Iraq and faced minimal opposition. Many Iraqi soldiers were said to have thrown down their weapons and ran or voluntarily surrendered rather than continue to fight. Iraq was considered defeated and expelled from Kuwait on February 28, 1991, thus ending Iraq's hopes of reclaiming Kuwait as its territory and gaining full access to Kuwait oil reserves. After U.S. experience three decades earlier in a prolonged war with Vietnam, all Americans wanted assurances from the President that we had a full plan not only for invasion but for extraction.

Many believed the U.N. coalition should have continued into Iraq and eliminated the threat of state sponsored terrorism, but Schwarzkopf is said to have opposed that action because victory was won and the uncertainties of what an invasion into Iraq might provoke from other Arab nations. President Bush had clearly demonstrated his ability to lead a wartime effort as Commander and Chief, to accomplish the mission, defeat the enemy, and withdraw military forces under the flag of victory. Memories are short, however, and much would be forgotten about his military leadership in the 1992 election.

By 1990, I realized it was time for me to begin looking towards the next step in my career. I had reached the position of GS-15 and the additional pay it brought, but we were still digging out of the financial straits of the move, having to buy a new vehicle for my commute and three times the house note we had left behind in Seabrook. I had fulfilled my commitment to come to D.C. for at least two years. I had just completed my third year and began looking for growth opportunities.

In the federal system, the Office of Personnel Management provides a formal training program to ready federal executives to enter the Senior Executive Service. President Jimmy Carter had asked Congress to create the SES as a replacement for the GS-16, 17 and 18 under the Civil Service Reform Act. The SES Act abolished those three grades and created a single pay band with tiers similar to the star ranks of the military. An entry level SES position would be equal to a Brigadier General and, likewise, a top tier SES position would be equal to a General (four stars). The Op.m. program is competitively advertised, and participants selected as if they were competing for a promotion. Upon selection to the class and completion of the training, the employee is eligible for promotion to the rank of SES without competition.

When I asked FWS Deputy Director Dick Smith if I should apply for the class, he said, "Of course. Don't you know you are next in our eyes?"

I didn't, but the boost of support meant everything to me. I applied for the Senior Executive Service Candidate Development Program (SESCDP) and was accepted. My 18 months of training would begin in early 1991, and I would be away from my normal duties off and on during that period. Each candidate was assured by their supervisor and the Director of the agency that they would be allowed to attend all activities considered part of the program curriculum. This program was considered the highest development priority for executives in the federal government.

During that same period, a friend of mine and Regional Director in Portland, Oregon had heavily recruited me to transfer to Portland as the Assistant Regional Director for Ecological Services, the program in which I had begun my career and gained some reputation working in wetlands. I was reluctant because of the SESCDP training, but Marv Plenert was insistent that he would fully support my training. That later proved to be conveniently forgotten, but the pressures of a job rather than integrity often drive decisions. John Turner had become Director of the FWS under President Bush and questioned why I would want to leave the relative calmness of my Fisheries position in D.C. and take what many would perceive as a step down to be an Assistant Regional Director. My counterpart in each region was the Deputy Regional Director, who supervised the position I would be accepting.

I explained to John that, even at the GS-15 grade and pay, Sarah and I couldn't afford a vacation unless it was to drive to relatives for a visit. I knew we would be financially better off away from the D.C. economy and hoped we would at least make enough on our Virginia home to have a down payment in Oregon. Second, Sarah was ready to have a little more financial security as well. Finally, I had come to fully recognize that the hand that was guiding me put opportunities in front of me to show the path I should be taking. I was compelled to make a difference in my career, and the issues of the northwest proved to be a fertile field for impact. Director Turner, a Wyoming resident and lifelong outdoorsman, said, "Okay. Let's see if you can stay on that bull for the full eight seconds."

He knew better than I what I was getting into. The next six years in our lives would bring the most stress I had ever faced.

CHAPTER 13:

Portland and the West

I left D.C. in January 1991, once again alone and saying tearful goodbyes to my family and drove the nearly 3,000 miles to Portland. Director Turner knew well the issues I was walking into. The northern spotted owl was heating to a boiling point under the Endangered Species Act and water shortages in the west continually created friction between legal mandates and the needs of people. I cover my time in Portland in detail in my book, COMPELLED, and encourage anyone interested in my experience with the evolution of the Endangered Species Act (ESA) and how western water law works to give it a read.

―――――

On October 3, 1991, Governor of Arkansas Bill Clinton announced his intention to run for President of the United States as the Democratic candidate. He had given the opening address for the Democratic National Convention in 1988, which had run for 33 minutes and was twice the time he had been allotted. Before becoming Governor of Arkansas, Clinton attended Georgetown University School of Foreign Service and was awarded a Rhodes Scholarship to University College Oxford, England, where he eventually cut his studies short and left without receiving a degree. From Oxford, he attended the Yale Law School and earned a law degree in 1973. During his college years, he was in open opposition to the Vietnam war and worked diligently to avoid military service. He returned home where he became a law professor at the University of Arkansas. As one of the youngest gubernatorial candidates in Arkansas history, Clinton was elected governor in 1978 at the age of 31. He served two stints as governor, one from 1979-1981, and another from 1983-1992.

During his first term as Governor, I worked closely with his staff, particularly David Criner, on wetland issues in Arkansas. The Clean Water Act allows a state to assume the Section 404 wetlands permit authority if it can demonstrate to the satisfaction of the EPA that it has the capability of properly administering the program in its state. Criner told Governor Clinton that I would be the right person to help them build a program and ensure compliance with the law. Under the Intergovernmental Personnel Act, employees from the federal government can be placed on detail with a state if benefits to the federal government can be shown.

Governor Clinton wrote a letter to Ken Black, Regional Director of the FWS at the time, requesting that I be allowed to work with the state to assist in the building of their program. Without either of them asking if I would like the assignment, Black wrote back and informed the Governor that I was one of the few Section 404 biologists he had to work all the lower Mississippi Valley, the only one working Arkansas, and the answer was, "No."

I don't know if it was something I would have wanted to do, but the question was resolved before Sarah and I were given the chance to think about it. Now, ten years later, that same young Governor was running for President of the United States. And he would play a significant role in the northwest forest issue.

Our luck in selling the house in Virginia went much better than our previous efforts, and it only took about three months, which allowed Sarah and the kids to join me when school let out for the summer. Sarah's sister, Fernell, continued her assistance in house hunting and the two of them found our next home on Nyssa Court in Beaverton, Oregon. My commute to work was Highway 26, also known as Sunset Highway, and took about a half hour. This "short" commute was an amazing gift after more than an hour drive each way in D.C. Erin, Adam, and Emily attended the Beaverton School District and loved their teachers and new friends. I was going through significant stress through the demands of the job, but I made sure my family was shielded from as much of that stress as possible. They loved it there, and I didn't want anything to interfere with that happiness.

My regional responsibilities included Oregon, Washington, California, Idaho, Nevada, and Hawaii. I was on the road most of the time because of the spotted owl, Klamath and California water issues, and the normal challenges of the remainder of the region. Erin adapted well to the new High School as Adam settled into middle school. Emily was thrilled to start her formal education and not be left at home each day. Erin was the social butterfly, easily making friends wherever she went and quickly became very popular in her school, enjoyed playing soccer and softball. We had the normal teenage issues of rebellion and seeking independence, but those were to be expected.

Sarah and I agreed it was time to add a new member to the family, so I asked my friend Dave Frederick for a recommendation on a family dog. Dave had moved to Olympia, Washington as the Field Supervisor while we were in D.C., and I was glad he was on the northwest team. He immediately said a black Labrador retriever, and it just so happened that his male had mated with a friend's female, and she had just had her litter. The kids had wanted a female so they could name her Nala, after the wildly popular movie *The Lion King*, but we ended up with a male and named him Simba.

Simba became the love of the house. He was gentle, loving, and playful. It seemed all he wanted to do was please us. I spent a considerable amount of time reading about dog training and working with him in our small backyard so he would be a hunting companion and retrieve harvested birds. I would throw the "bumper," a rubber tube that was a surrogate for a fallen bird, and he learned quickly to retrieve them. Unknown to me, Emily was watching from the sliding patio doors, and as soon as I went to work, she got Simba and the bumpers, threw them, and immediately started chasing Simba for them. Once the dog thinks it's a game, there is little chance one can return them to the "work" aspect of going hunting.

I, therefore, resigned myself to the idea that Simba would be a family dog and surrendered any hope he would hunt with me. That, by the way, was just fine with Emily. Adam was becoming quite the athlete. His major obstacle for football was his small size, a condition with which I could well identify. But baseball came naturally, and size didn't matter. He loved playing, and I was able to see a lot of his games because they were often on the weekends. He also played soccer and little league basketball, while doing very well in school.

We suffered another loss to the family in 1994, when our beloved Rubin Colwell passed away. He had lived nine years beyond Callie's death and never lost his love of his God, his country, nor his family. His death was difficult for me. He was the man that had instilled his love of "nadur" in me as a young boy, and I would not be able to attend the funeral due to geographic distance and work demands. But I silently told him I would do all I could in my life to nurture his nadur. It was a sad time.

My Appalachian Trail

I have never been one to bare my soul, probably because of a hill culture that encouraged keeping private things private. But going through the spotted owl critical habitat hearings and the other avalanche of demands was a whole new level of stress. By the end of 1995, I was beginning to feel the significant physical, as well as emotional, toll from the spotted owl, California water issues, and the herculean challenges our folks were facing from endangered species court settlements. For at least the last ten years, taking a vacation had become a luxury that many of us were seldom able to enjoy. A vacation became a four-day weekend or, at best, one week a year taken to go back east and visit family. Under the government system, annual leave can be accumulated to a certain amount, and then it must be taken or lost at the end of the year. I had been in "use or lose" for as long as I could remember, so every year around Christmas, when many of the issues seemed to slow down, I tried to use up as much of the leave that would be lost as I could. That was simply the norm.

In 1995, I had taken annual leave beginning on Thursday before Christmas all the way through the New Year's holiday. On Friday, December 20, I got up early and headed to the fitness club near our home in Beaverton as I usually did whenever not on travel. I had a good workout on my favorite NordicTrack ski machine and stepped over to the water fountain. When I swallowed the water, I felt a knot in my throat, much like one gets when air is trapped in the esophagus, but not as intense. I assumed I had swallowed air and was paying the price for drinking to rapidly. I tried to "walk it off," but it simply wouldn't go away. It was much more annoying than painful, so I was convinced it was spasms in my esophagus that would eventually subside. It didn't. I went down to the shower and then got in the jacuzzi to try and relax the muscles, still with no success.

I got dressed and arrived home just as Erin and Adam were leaving for their last day of school before the holiday break. Sarah was going to drop Emily off at school just a couple of blocks away, so I said, "I'll ride with you to drop Emily off and then we'll take a little ride."

"Where are we going?" she asked.

"I'll tell you after we drop Emily off."

As soon as Emily gave me a hug and got out of the minivan, Sarah said, "Okay, where are we going?"

I said we needed to go to the hospital because I was having a cramp in my throat and wanted to get it diagnosed.

She said in a highly worried voice, "Why didn't you tell me!?"

"That's why," I said. "I didn't want to frighten the children over something I think is minor."

We drove to the hospital, and I walked inside to the emergency room counter and told them I was having some pain in my "lower throat." The next thing I knew there was a hand on my shoulder pushing me down into a wheelchair and taking me back to a bed in the ER! I kept telling the nurse that I was fine and didn't think it was a heart attack, but I learned quickly that a patient's self-diagnosis is not a welcomed topic of discussion when there is "pain" at any level near the chest area. They gave me a nitroglycerin pill, the kind my father used to take, and constantly asked if it was helping. When I responded that it wasn't really making any difference, the nurse would ask, "On a scale of 1-10, how is the pain?"

"About a 3 or 4, and my ability to tolerate pain is high, so I don't feel distressed."

Instead of having the intended effect of lowering the concern, she simply said, "Okay, if you have a high tolerance for pain, it's probably a 6 or 7."

I gave up.

A cardiologist came in to see me and asked about the nitro pill, to which I responded that there had been no effect. He gave that some thought and told the nurse to give me another one. In about 10 minutes he came back to see how I was doing, and I said the pain had just gone away. He asked what I did for a living, and I told him I was a biologist. He then asked what I thought it was. I relayed that I believed I was having esophageal spasms and admitted that I really came in because I didn't want it to get worse and ruin my ability to enjoy Christmas and New Year's dinners!

He laughed, then said, "You might be right, but I want to keep you overnight for observation and to monitor your blood chemistry."

He left a prescription for a muscle relaxant in case it turned out I was correct and said his partner would check on me the next morning. As soon as the irritation was gone, I felt good enough to go work out again. But the hospital had different plans.

I spent the night being awakened every two hours by someone asking me if I was okay because my heart rate was so low. After they learned I worked out as often as I could, including running, they would smile and leave. Then, an hour later, someone would come take blood. A hospital is not a conducive place to get a good night's sleep. The next morning, they brought me a nice breakfast and told me I would likely be discharged after the cardiologist got there and checked me out. When the cardiologist arrived, the partner to the doctor I had spoken with the day before, he asked if I had breakfast yet. I knew where this was going.

"Yes, why?"

"Your cardiac enzymes were 'elevated,' not to the level of a heart attack, but more as a 'cardiac event.'"

I asked if he wanted to do an angioplasty to look around, and he said yes, but I could see he was worried. "I have a strong stomach. I won't aspirate on you."

He laughed and said, "I believe you. I'll have them come and prep you."

A couple of hours later, I was laying on an operating table with a screen next to my face where I could see my arteries and veins. I was allowed to stay awake for the procedure, which was one of the best gifts he could have given me. As a biologist, I got to watch the whole process on the screen as the small tip with a balloon was inserted in my femoral artery and worked its way up towards my chest. I was excited to see that my vascular system was clean and appeared to have no obstructions. When the tip reached my right coronary artery, I started to chuckle. He looked at me and said, "What's funny?"

"That's exactly how it hurt yesterday."

I had a significant amount of plaque buildup in that artery, and it was just to the point of starting to restrict enough blood flow to trigger a reaction. When he inflated the balloon to compress the plaque, he said, "This is very old and won't compress. We use the balloon to open the pathway and, if the plaque is soft, will stay flattened out. We'll have to put in a stint."

He explained that a stint was a very small metal tube inserted in the artery, then expanded to push the wall out and restore proper blood flow. "It sounds like a chicken wire culvert to me."

He laughed. "That's as good an explanation as any."

After the operation and another night in the hospital, he came to visit me in post op to give the okay for my release.

"What do you do for a living?"

"I'm a fish and wildlife biologist."

"Great! You're outside a lot in the woods and open areas."

"No. Unfortunately, I work in an office and am the lead Fish and Wildlife Service person for the northern spotted owl, endangered species, and other conservation issues."

He yelled out without thinking, "JESUS CHRIST, GET ANOTHER JOB!"

After he composed himself, he went on to say this was old plaque and the "event" was almost certainly brought on by stress.

When I got out of the hospital, I looked at my children and asked myself, "How much do I risk not being there for them and the special events in their lives?"

I had been at a high level of stress on the job for six years at that point. Being assigned another job in Portland with other responsibilities was out of the question due to the high profile of my current job and my name recognition associated with the issues. Whether I liked it or not, I was the name and face the public, Congress, the states, and the FWS expected to lead these controversial efforts. My involvement had included everything from working with the Congressional field staff to closed door sessions in offices of the White House. If I stayed in Portland, nothing would change. I loved the FWS too much to think about switching to another agency. The only alternative was to start exploring opportunities in other regions. Erin was in high school, and I intended to keep my promise to not move my children once they started 10th grade unless it was their idea. I could make that work if I timed it right, but the timing would have to be well-planned.

I spent a couple of weeks of convalescence at home on my back until I was no longer taking blood thinners. The major concern at that point was rupturing the entry point on my inner thigh and not being able to stop the bleeding. The major lesson I learned from my experience, and one I share with other men, is don't treat small pain as unimportant. We men are terrible about "walking it off" when we get chest pain, or saying, "It's just gas and will go away." The truth is, if I had been on the road when I got the throat spasms, I would have done just that, waited until it went away and got on with the day. I learned from the cardiologist that these small "cardiac events" are like tremors before an earthquake. Don't dismiss it; follow up on it. I know the hand of my Creator waited until I was home and in a position to act on it before he sent me the message. Once again, I was reminded I am never alone nor in charge.

I shared with my friends, Jerry Grover and now Regional Director Mike Spear, that I would eventually find a position elsewhere when Erin graduated to relieve the stress level, and they kept the secret well. We had lost Herman the previous January, and it was a blow to the whole family. Herman was not only the man that was more like a father to me than my own, but he was also a joy to be around. Always into something and always loving a joke. It was equally hard on our children, who were thousands of miles away from their two grandmothers. Jerry remained my right hand until he retired in March 1997 after 36 years of faithful service to the people of the United States.

Erin came to me and said she had been thinking about it and asked if there was any way we could move closer to her grandmothers. Momma was in southern Kentucky and Nell was in Louisiana, so I made a phone call to Atlanta to my friend Noreen Clough to ask her to keep me in mind if something came up. Noreen was the Regional Director and let me know that the Assistant Regional Director-Ecological Services would be open soon, and she would love to have me in that job. I had given up on ever getting an SES position. Even though I was eligible for promotion without competition, I was asked by the Director to apply for two separate SES jobs only to have someone else selected. Each time, I felt I had been kicked in the gut. I resolved myself to find a position and place where I would be happy finishing out my career, and Atlanta fit the bill perfectly. I went to Erin and relayed that there would soon be a position open in Atlanta, but it would be before she graduated from High School. She immediately said she wanted to move there, that she missed her cousins and grandmothers. I told her to think about it, that we had several months before we had to commit, and not rush to judgement.

About a month later, I got a call from John Rogers, FWS Deputy Director, telling me he felt I deserved a higher position than Assistant Regional Director and asked if I wouldn't prefer the job of Deputy Regional Director. The current deputy was moving to D.C., and that job would be available.

"Is Noreen okay with it?" I asked.

"Yes. She is all for it."

I said I would talk to my family and let him and Noreen know very soon. I went to Erin and asked her if she was still sure she wanted to move, even though it would make her finish high school in a new area where we didn't know anyone. I said, "Think about this very hard. Once I tell them yes, I'll keep my word."

Her response was immediate and firm. "Yes. I want to be closer to my grandmothers. I want to be where I can see them more often than once a year."

After talking with Sarah, I let John and Noreen know I would be pleased to move to Atlanta as the new Deputy Regional Director, GS-15. While the ARDs I would supervise had the same grade, my role would have higher authority than the one I currently occupied. In June 1997, I loaded my 1989 red Nissan hardbody pickup to the gills and headed back east. The time I spent in Atlanta without my family was much less on this move because the government had instituted a program of buy-out of your home if it didn't sell in a certain period of time. The offer might or might not be a good one, but you had an offer. It turned out the housing market was good in Portland, and we finally got a reasonable price for our house. Sarah and the kids followed shortly afterwards with a permanent move, but not before Sarah and her sister, Fernell, came on a house-hunting trip. It had become customary in all our moves for Fernell to accompany Sarah as they winnowed down the number of possible houses to the three they liked best. They would then ask me which one I liked, as if it mattered, and I dutifully did a verbal analysis of each and asked the right question: Which one had they decided on? As always, the priority was to find a good school district and then find a home in that district.

This time, Sarah and Fernell found a beautiful, newly constructed home in Snellville, Georgia, just outside Stone Mountain and only about a half-hour drive to work. Snellville's town motto is, "Everybody is somebody in Snellville." A perfect fit for us to settle in and finish my career. It was the first new home we ever owned, and I could ride the Stone Mountain freeway and never have to get on the choked-up I-75 or I-85. With the money we (finally) made on our house in Beaverton, we were able to get our beautiful home with nearly an acre of land with a creek flowing behind us for the kids to explore nature. As a bonus, we had an uneventful move with minimal separation time.

The fall of 1997 was the first time we had been able to get in a car and drive to see Momma or Nell in nearly seven years. Leland had contracted cancer in the late 1980s and ended his pain with a .38 revolver. I don't judge him for wanting to end the terminal suffering he was enduring, but he did it at their home in Ohio next to where my grandparents had moved, ensuring that my mother would be the one to find him. It seemed she was pre-ordained to care for sick and dying husbands. In the early 1990s, she struck up an old friendship with Roy Wooten, a fellow Kentuckian from the Hills, and they were married. They moved to a small community just outside Corbin, Kentucky, where they bought a home near Anna Lee and her new husband, "Red" Grizzle. It was only a five-hour drive to visit them, a true luxury compared to a trip from Oregon.

After Herman's death, Nell was living alone in Bunkie but was surrounded by friends and family. Melvin dropped in almost daily to see how she was doing. That gave Sarah, Phyllis, and Fernell some comfort, since they lived several hours to a day's drive from their old hometown. But the move to Atlanta allowed us to visit our mothers on a much more frequent basis. Christmas in 1997 brought all of Nell's children to be around her for only the second Christmas since Herman had died. The home was filled with love. Because Erin had taken advanced classes, she graduated from South Gwinnett High School in December and began her efforts for enrollment at LSU for the fall semester, 1998. Baton Rouge is only an hour and a half from Bunkie, which would allow her to regularly visit with her grandmother on weekends.

CHAPTER 14:

The Southeast and More Time with Family

Our home in Snellville, Georgia on the northeast outskirts of Atlanta was, by far, the best house we had ever owned. Our home on Nyssa Court in Beaverton, just east of Portland, was in a nice neighborhood with good neighbors, but the home was modest, with approximately 1,800 square feet and a small front and back yard. The house in Rutledge Manor in Snellville was almost 2,700 square feet and had three quarters of an acre, with much of it wooded and a small stream for the kids to explore nature. Sarah and Fernell had done well, and we were settled in by the time school started in the fall of 1997. Being the Deputy Regional Director (DRD) gave me the opportunity to keep a low profile while still having the ability to influence decisions.

Erin only needed one more semester in high school to graduate and enrolled at South Gwinnett High School. She graduated with honors by December and began preparing for College at LSU the next fall. She would finally be where she could simply drive the one and a half hours from Baton Rouge to Bunkie and spend the weekend with Nell any time she wanted. Erin continued her role as a social butterfly and quickly made friends wherever she was. She was headstrong, independent yet still frail, and always knew what she wanted to do with her life, even if it changed frequently! However, she was never shy about working to have the extra money she wanted for her social activities and extra gas money for the Mitsubishi Mirage her mother and I bought her. I make no judgements for the behavior of any of my children, especially given the lack of direction and behavior I exhibited in my first year of college and most of the time I was in the Air Force.

Adam was very active in baseball and soccer, which allowed his small size to not be a disadvantage. His years in middle school reinforced his desire to be involved in sports, but it was too early to determine which one(s) would be the focus. His allergies expanded significantly by moving to the southeastern U.S. where pollen is prevalent. We almost immediately had to begin shot treatments with his allergist and restrict animals and other pollen-carriers from his bedroom. With the added pollens of the south, Simba was banned from Adam's bedroom and restricted to the downstairs.

Emily was the princess of the house, just beginning to get involved in soccer. Her soccer coach, Coach Jim, had been a semi-professional soccer player, and I'm not sure there could have been any room in him for more energy and enthusiasm. Emily loved Coach Jim. Therefore, so did we. We discovered she was quite good at the game and loved the nickname Coach Jim gave her, MC, short for Mrs. Clause. He dubbed her so because her birthday is December 29 and very close to Christmas. She also discovered her enjoyment of the stage when her class put on a rendition of *The Sound of Music*. Her role was as a grip backstage, and she loved it! My ability to actually attend these things in the lives of my children was a godsend. The demands of my job in Portland and the western U.S. had all but eclipsed my ability to attend Erin's softball and soccer games and be there for the things important in her life.

The low demands for travel as the DRD freed me to attend nearly *every* important school and social event in Adam and Emily's life. I also bought my first boat from Sarah's brother, Melvin, which was a 16.5 ft Spirit bass boat with an 85 horsepower Yamaha outboard motor. Lake

Oconee was just east of Snellville near Conyers and made it easy to create family memories that I still carry today. Both Adam and Emily loved to fish, so I not only got to enjoy the pastime I had done all my life but got to teach my children the love of nature, being on the water, and the importance of conservation. Emily liked to be pulled in the innertube, as did Adam, but Adam also became quite adept with a wakeboard. Sarah would often join us, and when Erin visited from college in the summer, we were all able to go as a family.

Adam found the sport he loved in 9th grade. Of all sports, wrestling focuses the most on specific size and weight levels. No longer was the boy that was smaller than many others his age forced to compete on an unlevel playing field. Adam had the athletic ability to play football and basketball, but he also had his father's developmental trajectory. Just as I had been small until I reached my post teens, Adam was also small. Wrestling, however, allowed him to compete against other boys who also weighed 102 pounds. Beginning immediately in 9th grade, he excelled. I became the team photographer, and Sarah and I both attended nearly every match and tournament and have the callouses on our gluteus maxima from sitting hours on end in the stands waiting for his turn to wrestle to show for it! But it was all worth it. I was able to be there for Adam and Emily as I had not been able to be there for Erin in her high school years. My time as Dad was finally equal to my time as a professional. Life was good.

The final disappointment of my career came when Noreen Clough, Regional Director in Atlanta, told me immediately upon my arrival that she was going to retire in one month! I was stepping into the Deputy Regional Director's position and would only have the benefit of Noreen's counsel for one month. As a graduate of the Senior Executive Service Candidate Development Program, I was eligible for promotion to the SES and as Regional Director with just the signature of the Director. I told myself I had no right to believe I would be promoted, especially since our new Director, Jamie Clark, and I did not see eye to eye on conservation approaches. But I was unsuccessful at pushing my hopes away. When Jamie selected Sam Hamilton, a man whom I respected but was also an Assistant Regional Director that reported to me, I felt another huge kick in my gut. Over the years, when I was faced with disappointment and apparent failure in my efforts, I returned to a famous quote from Theodore Roosevelt about trial and struggle.

> "It is not the critic who counts. Not the man who points out how the strong Man stumbled, or where the doers of deeds could have done them better.
>
> The credit belongs to the man who is actually in the arena, whose face is marred by the dust and sweat and blood; who strives valiantly, who errs and comes short again and again...who knows the great enthusiasms, the great devotions, and spends himself in a worthy cause; who, at the best, knows in the end the triumph of high achievement; and who, at the worst, if he fails, at least fails while daring greatly, so that his place shall never be with those cold and timid souls who know neither victory nor defeat."

I had stumbled and tasted the dust and blood of failure. I had learned that I had no choice but to get up, take a deep breath, and continue giving nothing but my best effort. I knew others were watching me fail, but it didn't matter. I was compelled to continue. I resolved that the only way anyone could be defeated is to surrender and, as Winston Churchill famously told the people of Great Britain when Hitler was at their doorstep, "We will never surrender." I was again reminded that it is not how I view my works or talents; it is how others view them that will determine whether I am deemed worthy of promotion.

However, it is *my* responsibility to determine how I deal with failure. I recommitted to simply doing the best I could in the job I was blessed to have and cease expectations about future promotions once and for all, and to enjoy spending the remainder of my career working with people

I respected. My intention was to be the best Deputy Regional Director I could be, finish my career with dignity and gratitude for what I had been given, and enjoy my family. Once again, I placed my faith in the hand that was guiding me. Sam, however, treated me with dignity and respect for the experience I had gained, and we worked as well together as any two could have. When Steve Thompson and Mitch King joined us in the Regional Office, we had a strong team. Cindy Dohner was growing quickly into the leader we knew she could be, and my role was mostly to guide and support the team. That gave me more time home than I had since being field supervisor in Clear Lake. Sam could not have been more gracious in asking for my support and never treated me as less than an equal in running the Region.

After Sam had been promoted over me to be the Regional Director, I had fully settled in my mind that I would never achieve the rank of Senior Executive Service, that those things were out of my control, and I believed the hand that was guiding my life intended me to retire as the DRD of the Southeast Region. But, as usual, I was neither in charge of my life nor destiny, and I would soon be reminded of that fact. In November 2000, Sam called me into his office for a phone call with Director Jamie Rappaport Clark. This was not unusual. Except for very confidential or pre-decisional discussions, Sam included me in all calls with the Director, especially when she was asking for advice on things pertaining to our Region. But this call was different. Jamie got right to the point and said, "I want to congratulate you on becoming one of the first two Deputy Regional Directors to have the rank of SES. I have obtained permission to promote you and Rowan Gould (in Alaska) as the first two deputies with SES rank."

To say I was stunned would be an understatement. Over the years, Jamie and I had not seen eye to eye on approaches to conservation, especially the Endangered Species Act. She very strongly endorsed regulations and using the weight of the law to approach ESA issues, while I had learned the hard way that regulatory "wins" only last as long as the views of the current party remained in control. Then the pendulum swings to the other side. I had learned that the only real power any of us has is that which we share. Therefore, the most important tools for seeing that species don't go extinct in the U.S. are those that can eliminate the threats *before* the species is pushed to the brink of extinction. For Jamie to overlook our different points of view and accept Sam's recommenddation that I be promoted spoke to Jamie's character and professionalism. I was officially a member of the Senior Executive Service of the United States government.

George W. Bush asked Dick Cheney to lead the search for his Vice-Presidential running mate, and ultimately decided to offer the job to Cheney. They were on the Republican ticket, and Al Gore selected Joe Lieberman to be his running mate for the Democratic Party. The election was one of the closest in history, with Florida as the deciding state by only a few hundred votes. The election was contested in both the Florida Supreme Court and the U.S. Supreme Court. On December 12, 2000, the U.S. Supreme Court decided in favor of Bush and Vice President Gore conceded that the Florida electoral college votes would put Bush over for the win. It will forever be known as the "hanging chad election" because of the questionable votes cast by pushing a hole through a "chad" on the ballot to indicate their selection. Both Gore and Bush were magnanimous in their behavior towards the other, with pledges to work together for the good of the country. Bush would become President in January of 2001.

About a year later, on December 7, 2001, Sam Hamilton had called for a regional directorate retreat at his community clubhouse in Lawrenceville. We had these retreats about every quarter to have the luxury of spending time with each other as both friends and a team. We discussed strategies and directions we needed to be taking and were free from anything except emergency phone calls. Sam came to me at a morning break and said he had just received a message from FWS Deputy Director Marshall Jones asking me to call him at 2 p.m. that afternoon. I asked what it was about, and Sam responded that he wasn't sure. But I sensed that might not be the case. I called Marshall at the appointed time, and the conversation began with the following:

"Hi, Dale. I have something I need you to do for us."

"Sure, Marshall," I said. "What is it?"

"I need you to go to Albuquerque as the Acting Regional Director."

"You have a Regional Director in place there. Do you have Nancy doing something else? How long do you think it will last?" I said.

"Either a few months or permanently," he said in a serious voice.

As a member of the SES, I had accepted the obligations to report to any position or duty station I was assigned and be there within ninety days with no recourse for refusal except resignation. Those are the rules of the SES. There are certain benefits in annual leave and pay that also come with the rank, but the obligation I accepted with the rank was to follow Marshall's request ... or resign. I was not keen on moving my family again, but my word is my word.

When I returned to the meeting, Sam had already told the regional directorate that I was headed to Albuquerque as the Acting, and most likely permanent, Regional Director. He tossed me a T-shirt with "Region 2, The Southwest Region" written on it, and his smile could not have been more genuine. I left for my first visit to Albuquerque before Christmas and returned for the long haul right after the holidays. I was quickly told by Marshall and David Smith, Principal Deputy Assistant Secretary for Fish, Wildlife and Parks, that it would be permanent, and I should start planning on bringing my family to New

Mexico. However, much like the military, nothing happens in the government unless there are orders printed, signed, and delivered. I had none.

When June rolled around and everyone treated me as the Regional Director, including and up to the Secretary, I still didn't have orders. Technically, I had exceeded the maximum 120 days that I could be in the position without having received formal papers. I had spent the last six months in Albuquerque without my family and had missed being there for the last semester of Adam's senior year. This gave me the ability to call Marshall and say I did not intend to return to Albuquerque after I went home to visit my family over the 4th of July holiday unless I had orders in hand.

I said I had promised my children I would not move them after they started their first day of 10th grade, and Emily would be in school starting in September. I relayed that I would not pull her out of school to move her, and therefore I would not move, unless it happened before September. We needed at least 60 days to move them there, so the clock was ticking. Even as a member of the SES, I could not be left hanging in limbo for that long. Marshall agreed and said my orders had been in the Assistant Secretary's office for three months. I thanked him, called Deputy Assistant Secretary David P. Smith, and relayed the same warning I had given Marshall.

He immediately apologized and said he would hand-walk the papers through the department that day, and he did! I had official orders assigning me as the Regional Director, Southwest Region, Albuquerque, New Mexico in hand by the time I flew home for the 4th of July holiday and Sarah's birthday on the 10th. It was official. Adam had graduated from South Gwinnett High School in May and was enrolled at Georgia Tech for the fall semester. Sarah, Emily, and I would be living in Albuquerque.

CHAPTER 15:

New Mexico and the Southwest

When Sarah, Fernell, and Emily came for a house hunting trip, we moved into temporary quarters near Emily's new school in Rio Rancho. Adam prepared to begin college at Georgia Tech, where he hoped to gain an understanding of engineering. His thought at the time was to become a patent attorney and to work with entrepreneurs bringing the latest inventions to the business world. When the official announcement of my new assignment was made, the FWS family let me know they were with me through the stack of notes and congratulatory emails I received. I was officially the Regional Director of the Southwest Region but had spent six months without my family in Adam's senior year. But I had fulfilled my obligation as a member of the SES and had moved where the FWS needed me. Sarah, Emily, and I were New Mexico's newest residents.

When school began, Emily made new friends quickly and easily settled into a new life in the southwest. The climate in Rio Rancho was much different than Atlanta. There were four very distinct seasons, extremely low humidity, and less rainfall than anywhere we had previously lived. Albuquerque sits with the Sandia Mountains on the east side that have an elevation of 10,679 feet mean sea level, with Albuquerque at just over 5,000 feet. An hour up the road, Santa Fe is just over a mile high and is very near the Sandia Laboratories, which are well known for their work in nuclear research, both for energy and national security.

The Rio Grande River runs through the middle of downtown Albuquerque, and the forested area along the river is called the "bosque" (boss-k), a Spanish term for forested floodplains. While the floods of the southwest seldom reach the scope and breadth of those in the southeast, the biological functions are very similar. The bosque serves much like Central Park does for New Yorkers, giving space and trails for hiking and jogging. The change in population was also noticeable. We left the Atlanta Metropolitan area that had more than three million people to settle in New Mexico, which only had about two million in the entire state. It was nice to be in towns that were small enough to get to know the people, yet large enough to have all the amenities.

Sarah settled in quickly, thanks in large part to our old friends, Pat and Floyd Nudi. Pat was a wealth of information about the area, where to find the best shopping and things to do when I was travelling for work. Sarah is an outgoing person and quickly makes friends. Soon, she knew everyone on our street. She continued to work as a volunteer at Emily's school, help with shuttling kids to and from athletic practices and games, and generally doing whatever she could to help keep Emily's life going smoothly. Emily continued her love of soccer and also engaged more in the Thespian Club, honing her skills as an actor and stagehand. While Emily had her occasions when discipline was in order, she was generally well behaved for a teenager and gave us very little cause for stress. She had learned from her older siblings how to make her mistakes in private ... most of the time.

Erin was doing well at LSU working on a Bachelor of Science degree in Psychology. She had joined a sorority and was fully engaged in the social activities of life on campus. Adam was finding his way as a new freshman at Georgia Tech and, much as I had done, trying to figure out how to navigate a very large university where no one pushed you to get your work done. My life at the Regional Office had almost become normal since I had been there for over seven months. I was learning much about the issues of western water once again, with the Rio Grande being the primary focus in New Mexico and the Lower Colorado River in Arizona.

My time in Portland had prepared me well for the expectations of water users and the scarcity of this liquid gold. My first real challenge dealt with the biological opinion under the Endangered Species Act (ESA) for the endangered silvery minnow (*Hybognathus amarus*), along the Albuquerque stretch of the Middle Rio Grande River. Any federal agency undertaking an action which might either harm a listed species or place the species in jeopardy of extinction must consult with the U.S. Fish and Wildlife Service and receive a biological opinion regarding the action. If there will be take (harm), the agency must receive authorization from the FWS. If the action might place the species in jeopardy of extinction, the action cannot be carried out as planned.

The FWS must, if available, provide a reasonable and prudent alternative to the planned action that would remove the threat of jeopardy. One of the first issues I faced as the new Regional Director was to testify in a trial where we (the FWS) believed there was no escaping a jeopardy situation, even if no action was taken. The court case that ensued resulted in new conservation law being made. The court ruled, and the appellate court agreed, that the Endangered Species Act took priority over all other contracts the Bureau of Reclamation administered. That placed the ESA above what had become known as "western water rights," which were contracts with the Bureau to deliver water to farms and cities and changed the way water rights were viewed under the ESA.

The area of responsibility for the southwest region included Texas, Oklahoma, Arizona, and New Mexico. At that time, some of the most powerful members of congress were found there. Senators Pete Dominici (R-NM), Jeff Bingaman (D-NM), John McCain (R-AZ), James Inhoffe (R-OK), John Cornyn (R-TX), and Kay Bailey Hutchinson (R-TX). With the election of George W. Bush as president, this meant there was a stronghold of Republican power in my region, and it drew more than a little attention from Director Steve Williams, Assistant Secretary for

Fish, Wildlife and Parks Craig Manson, Deputy Secretary Steven Griles, and Secretary Gale Norton.

Fortunately, my approach to conservation was staunchly based in working with our partners in the states, non-governmental organizations, and the public. I had learned much during my time working the northern spotted owl and California water issues and knew the only real power any of us possess is that which we share and allow to grow. By doing this, I learned that sharing cultivates respect, and from respect emerges trust. Without trust, no team can survive. With trust, there is no limit to team potential. All senators both Republican and Democrat in the southwest fully supported that philosophy.

Another challenge that emerged during the droughts of the early 2000s in the southwest was that of water distribution along the Colorado River. The Colorado River compact was signed at the end of the highest level of river flows on record. As a result, it became nearly impossible to meet the demands of the compact and deliver water to each state and Mexico, as called for in the agreement. The problem stemmed from flows that measured over 16 million acre-feet (the amount of water needed to cover one acre of ground to a depth of one foot, or 325,850 gallons) that flowed down the river the year before the compact was signed, and the *real* average flow of approximately 13 million acre-feet per year.

The compact has seven states, four in the upper basin and three in the lower basin. New Mexico, Arizona, and California were the three states at the bottom of the system, and two of them were in my region. However, I was able to help work with all three states, and the numerous water contractors, to reach an agreement that provided specific levels of water to each state in return for $620 million in habitat and river conservation. That decision required me to go against the legal advice I was receiving and place trust in our state partners to deliver what they promised. While some criticized me for being willing to share the power of the permit program, I knew there was little risk for the American people. The one authority that could not be delegated was the oversight of the permit and the ability to withdraw authorization at any point the states did not fulfill their obligations. All parties knew this, but it was never spoken.

After several issues similar to the Lower Colorado River and silvery minnow, including a directive to lead a team of biologists to do the ESA biological opinion on the Missouri River, I received a phone call from the Deputy Assistant Secretary of the Interior for Fish, Wildlife and Parks. David P. Smith had become a good friend through working the issues, and I thought nothing of him calling me on any given day to discuss issues and possible solutions. On this day, he called to ask if I would agree to let Assistant Secretary Craig Manson put my name in consideration to be the Director of the FWS. Steve Williams had just vacated the position to assume the role of CEO of the Wildlife Management Institute. It was common to submit a member of the FWS team to be considered for the position of Director, but there had not been a career employee appointed as Director since Lynn Greenwalt under the Nixon Administration.

I smiled over the phone and said I would be honored. My thought was that I had simply been the one chosen this time to say they looked inside the FWS, looked outside, and ended up going outside. That's the way it had been for thirty years. When I received the surprising phone call to come to Washington, D.C. for an interview with the Secretary, then later to have an interview with the White House, it went from surprise to shock! I really didn't want the job. It paid the same as my current position, I would have to go to D.C. alone until Emily graduated in order to keep my promise of not moving her after beginning 10th grade, and I hadn't even really talked to Sarah about it. I was advised by Chief of Staff for the Secretary, Brian Waidmann, that I had better talk to Sarah because the wheels were rolling. I went home to have that discussion.

I told Sarah I would have to go to D.C. without her and Emily until Emily graduated, only see them whenever I could work it out, and it would increase our bills to pay for a small apartment in D.C. I was hoping she would be my way out and say, "We can't do that."

Instead, Sarah said, "We can make that work."

We can make that work? I was floored. Then, she reminded me of all the reasons the FWS needed someone who knew the issues, the people, and the culture. Before she was finished, I realized there was only one ethical choice if I were selected. When Emily got home from school and I filled her in, she asked, "Will I have to move?" I said, "No, but I won't be able to live with you and your mom for nearly two years until you graduate."

She said, "Okay. I'm good with it then."

The jury had spoken.

I received the mountain of paperwork on my background, our finances, any drug or alcohol problems, domestic help, etc. I think they knew how many hemorrhoids I had by the time everything was done. The only thing I was not asked before the President decided to nominate me for the position was my political party affiliation. I was amazed by that. Every previous administration had sent the strong message that all political appointees had to demonstrate significant party support over the years. President Bush apparently didn't care. He thought I was the right person because of the way I viewed the issues, and that was enough. That made my respect for him grow even more.

I was nominated by the President in July 2005 and confirmed by the Senate by unanimous agreement one day after my nomination left the Senate Environment and Public Works Committee. The President signed my official appointment documents on October 12, 2005. I loaded my 1989 Nissan Hardbody pickup truck with all it would hold, pulled a U-Haul trailer with the meager furniture I would need to live alone in D.C., and headed back to the east coast.

CHAPTER 16:

The Director and Virginia

My first day on the job, I was sworn in by Secretary of the Interior Gale Norton in a private ceremony to officially have me able to perform the duties of the job. The formal swearing-in ceremony would be held on November 3rd, my fifty-sixth birthday. I started making plans to invite friends and family that could make it. I called Momma as soon as we set the date and told her how much I looked forward to having her there. I knew they couldn't drive all day at their age, so I assured her that Sarah and I would buy airline tickets for her and Roy.

She called me the next day to say they would not be able to come. Apparently, Roy was afraid of flying after 9/11. I told her I understood that Roy wouldn't come, but she would, right?

"No, honey. I just can't leave him here with nobody to look after him."

"Momma, he's a grown man and can either cook his own meals or eat out. This is the most important day in my professional life. I want you here and, frankly, don't care if Roy comes or not. He has no right to make you feel bad about coming alone."

She replied, "I'm sorry, Dale. I would just feel too bad leaving him here."

To be clear, there was nothing wrong with Roy's health that would prohibit him from taking care of himself for three days. He simply thought Momma should be there to fix his meals and attend to his needs. To say I was angry and disappointed would be an understatement.

I accepted her answer. She was an adult and could decide for herself. I have no doubt she didn't understand the significance of the ceremony. In all my life, I'm not sure I ever witnessed a more selfish act than Roy Wooten displayed. It is a good thing she wouldn't let me talk to him on the phone. I never got over my disgust for Roy after that. When she sent my birthday card, it had an extra hand-written note.

"Dale, honey, I sure wish I was there. There isn't anyone in this world that wants to be there more than me. I will be thinking of you all day. Will try to call you that night on your cell phone. Love you and proud to have you for my son. Thank God for you. Love Always. Mom XO."

While Momma couldn't be there, I was surrounded by my immediate family and a host of friends. Erin brought a friend from New Orleans, Adam brought his childhood friend from Snellville, and Emily flew in with Sarah. Richard and Fernell Cryar were the only other family members that could make it, and I was greatly appreciative. Our old friends, Mitch and Carla King, were there, as well as my wonderful friend and mentor, Lynn Greenwalt, and his beautiful wife, Judy. Lynn had been the last person to be appointed Director of the FWS as a career FWS employee. There had been thirty years of separation between his appointment and mine. It was important to me that they be there to show the culture and connection of the FWS family.

Sarah, Erin, Adam, and Emily made me proud. As I looked at my children, I saw the young adults I knew they could be. Erin had survived Hurricane Katrina and being trapped in the hospital. Adam had transferred to Georgia Southern pursuing a degree in Criminal Justice, and Emily was becoming a beautiful young lady. Of course, having Sarah hold the Bible as I took the oath of office was beyond satisfying. I felt nothing but love and support.

On February 14, 2006, three months after my official swearing-in, I was in a meeting with Secretary Norton when my Executive Assistant walked into the room and said, "Dale, your mother has been in an automobile accident."

Gale looked at me and said, "Go do whatever you need to do for your mother. Let us know if you need anything at all."

I learned that Roy, whose eyesight was so bad he could not pass the test to renew his driver's license, had insisted on driving into Corbin to get supplies and medicine. As they were pulling out of the parking lot of the pharmacy, Momma had not completed buckling her seatbelt when Roy pulled out in front of a young girl, causing her to hit Roy's truck on the driver's side. The impact threw Momma across the truck, and her head hit the steering wheel and gear shift. While she was not dead upon impact, for all practical purposes, she was. That same person who couldn't possibly deal with being left alone for three days while Momma attended my swearing-in ceremony had just killed her through his pride and neglect.

There is no adequate description for the shock and horror I felt. Sarah, Erin, and Emily flew into Knoxville, Tennessee. Sarah and Emily rented a car, and Adam picked up Erin on his way up from Atlanta. I was feeling the pain of separation from my family more deeply while I made the drive from Virginia to Corbin through the night. I'm not sure I felt whole again until two years later when Sarah finally joined me in Virginia, and we bought a home there. I thought throughout the night of the joys Daddy refused because he was afraid of dying before Larry reached his 18th birthday, and how Momma was healthy and happy for a 78 year old, only to die in a car accident. My resolve to accept each day as a gift from the Creator and use it to the best purposes I could became even stronger.

After the funeral, we all returned to our lives, but emptier with Momma gone. Emily continued to do well in school and graduated in 2007. Adam struggled finding himself, much as I had done, but didn't have the benefit of the Air Force to help mold him into an adult. My greatest loss in the first two years of time as the Director was within my family. Of all the children that had put up with so much of my absence, Emily paid the highest price. When I reported for duty in October 2005, it was the beginning of Emily's 11th grade. I was able to be there for almost none of the special moments in her life for two full school years. The quick answer of, "As long as I don't have to move, it's okay if you go to D.C.," became more regretful as it dawned on her that I was significantly bound to the responsibilities of my job and couldn't get home as much as I wanted. I missed nearly all of Emily's Thespian Club activities and plays. I would always call and ask how it went, but that wasn't the same as being there for her. Following Emily's graduation and acceptance at LSU, Sarah and I began looking for a home in Virginia where we could be together again. We had little trouble selling our house in Rio Rancho and had a reasonable down payment for a home in Virginia.

For the first time in our married life, we didn't have to worry about finding a good school and then finding a home. We were free to find a home that allowed the most benefits to Sarah for her settling in and for my commute to work. The federal government offered a subsidy to any employee who would reduce highway traffic and commute via mass transit. As Director of the FWS, I was entitled to a free parking space in the basement of the Department of the Interior building where we worked. However, I had vivid memories of the horrible traffic in Washington, D.C. from my first tour of duty in the late 1980s and knew it would only be worse in 2007. I declined the offer of the free parking space and elected to receive the mass transit subsidy. The METRO in Washington is a high-quality means of transportation, usually on time and always clean and safe. I also liked the decompression time on my ride home to Springfield, where we bought a nice town home just a couple of miles from the METRO station. Between the subsidy and the heavy travel of the Director, my commute was almost free. However, the look on the face of the staff person that brought me my parking pass, only to have me tell them I would ride the METRO instead, was priceless! Turning down a parking space in Washington, D.C. just didn't happen!

Sarah, Emily, and our wonderful black Labrador, Simba (a 97-pound bundle of love and devotion), survived well enough, but we all knew a big piece of family memories had been missed. Those are family sacrifices made in public service that seldom get recognized. Emily graduated from Rio Rancho High School in 2007 and set her sights on college at LSU. With the Metro subsidy, I wanted to be where it was easy to get to the train, yet as far out of D.C. as I could for the personal time. We found a townhome in Springfield, Virginia near the METRO station. An added bonus was in finding wonderful neighbors next door in Tony and Annette Koelker, and a couple of houses down were Air Force Officers Riggs and Teri Riggleman. My 22-month stint alone in an apartment was finally over, and I could enjoy having a real home and Sarah with me once again.

Adam had settled into life at Georgia Southern, and a new life was in Erin's future. In the spring of 2008, she decided to take advantage of being single and went to California for 13 weeks as a "traveling nurse." New Orleans was still in the recovery mode from Hurricane Katrina, and at least 200,000 people that evacuated during the storm had not returned. The New Orleans hospital agreed to let Erin do the travelling nurse experience while things were slowly getting back to normal. Little did we know, those 13 weeks would turn into years when she was lured to stay by her newfound love for California and an emergency room physician that would become our son-in-law in 2012. Sarah and I were pleased that our children were doing well but didn't like how difficult it was to get together. I told Sarah, "We raised them to be independent and not afraid to take on new adventures. I guess it worked."

We lived on John Rylands Way in Springfield and had wonderful neighbors in our little cul-de-sac. Along with the Koelkers and Rigglemans were John and Dee Dee Fusco at the end of the street. All our neighbors became close friends, and we still keep in touch with them today. Tony was an executive in a private company that oversaw hospital and medical treatment of military personnel. To say he was committed to taking care of our men and women in uniform would be a gross understatement. Sarah became very close friends with Annette, as I did with Tony.

It would not be accurate to say my time as Director was "fun." As Steve Williams before me had said, "By the time the issue gets to my desk, it can't be solved."

I wouldn't totally agree with that statement, but they are certainly entrenched in controversy. The two most memorable issues we faced were the listing of the polar bear as the first species listed under the Endangered Species Act due to global warming. The second was the laying to rest of the Yazoo Backwater Pumps Project, a monstrosity that had been under study for sixty years but was just too damaging to the natural resources to ever be approved. When I look back on my time as Director, however, my memories are not of the painful controversies, but rather of the wonderful, dedicated professionals that I was honored to work with and lead. It is because of them, and all of the people that are called to be involved in conservation, that I named the book about my career "COMPELLED." The most common thread among conservationists is their belief that they have no moral choice except to be involved. Their gift of devotion to the resources we love is all the reward I needed.

As it was getting close to the end of the second term for President Bush, I realized that I would have to leave my politically appointed position and chose to retire rather than exercise my right to go back into the ranks of government as a senior executive. Under the law, because I had no break in service when going from the career rank of SES to the rank of Director, I was entitled to return to the career ranks. However, that never works. Once one has taken the step from career to political appointee, there is realistically no way back. I retired from the FWS after more than thirty years as a civilian and four years in the military. With a full year of unused sick leave that counted as "good time," I retired with thirty-five years of service to my country. I had taken the oath to preserve and defend the constitution of the United States three times: when I entered the military, when I entered the civilian ranks of the federal government, and when I became Director. That commitment to my God and my country has been, and remains, non-negotiable.

I began to get phone calls right away asking if I would be a consultant and go "on retainer" with various entities. I was also asked if I would be interested in being the CEO of a couple of conservation organizations but declined because I promised Sarah I wouldn't go back to work full-time again. I eventually accepted consultation requests from the National Fish and Wildlife Foundation and the Association of Fish and Wildlife Agencies, the organization that represents all state fish and wildlife agencies. Then another, and another, and another. Within six months, I was working full-time! That was not my intent, so I worked to drop a couple, which had me working about three days a week. Then, in December 2009, I got a call from Ducks Unlimited.

CHAPTER 17:

Ducks Unlimited

It was a December evening and typically cold in northern Virginia. I had done some work that day for my clients and had gone to the kitchen to heat up some leftovers for supper. Sarah was watching the news as I put a dish in the microwave. My cell phone rang, and I answered it. On the other end was Dan Sherman, an executive recruiter I knew because of his work in California when Sarah and I lived in Portland. After the pleasantries of family and health were covered, he said he was hired by Ducks Unlimited (DU) to find a new CEO. I had heard that Don Young had abruptly left DU around August, which normally means it wasn't voluntary, and assumed he was calling to ask if I knew anyone that I might be able to recommend. I was used to getting these calls because of the people I had come to know through the course of my career. Instead, he asked if I would be interested the position. I was a bit shocked because he knew from previous discussions that I had declined other offers of this nature. I had promised Sarah I wouldn't work full-time again but was always ready to help anyone I could to advance conservation.

The difference this time was we were discussing Ducks Unlimited, the largest and most successful wetlands and waterfowl conservation organization in the world. As I agreed to have discussions with the search committee, Sarah said, "Well, I guess we're moving again."

I insisted that I had only agreed to talk with them, and they had made no such offer. Her response was, "We're moving."

After much discussion and two interviews later, I accepted the position of CEO of Ducks Unlimited and reported for duty on May 3, 2010.

Sarah and I moved into our new home in Collierville just outside of Memphis in October, and Sarah quickly learned to love the DU "family." For the first time in our lives, she was able to attend events and get to know the wonderful volunteers and staff that I had known throughout my career. Just as with the dedicated people I had known in government, the conservationists at Ducks Unlimited truly excelled in their love of the resource first and enjoying hunting and other activities only after the conservation mission had been secured. It was a theme I had witnessed over and over again. People in conservation are compelled to give back and ensure future generations inherit the great natural riches that we were able to enjoy. It also allowed Sarah to be within a seven-hour drive of Bunkie to help take care of Nell, whose health was deteriorating.

The staff at DU were wonderful, with very few exceptions. Just as with any company, there are the occasional individuals that betrayed the trust of their colleagues and were appropriately dealt with. But that was extremely rare. In nine years as the CEO, I can recall less than four instances where a member of the 40,000+ volunteers ever asked for anything in return for their work and dedication to the mission. At DU, no board member nor volunteer is ever reimbursed for expenses incurred in the service of the company. Instead, all volunteers give many hours of effort to put on over 4,000 events each year to "raise money for the ducks." This catchphrase is shorthand for creating hundreds of thousands of acres of wetlands and waterfowl habitat each year. Of course, ducks and geese are not the only beneficiaries. For each wetland restoration project completed, the U.S. Fish and Wildlife Service estimates that over 700 species received benefit; indeed, the entire micro-ecosystem is enhanced.

The board of directors bear their own expenses to board meetings, events, and the state and national conventions. The volunteer president of Ducks Unlimited will easily spend $30,000 to $40,000 each year of their two-year presidency satisfying the duties of their office. No expenses are covered by DU. In addition, volunteers make generous donations, many have land holdings they manage as wetlands, and all have a very generous heart. Once again, I was reminded that people involved in conservation are dedicated to giving back, not taking. The most constant question I heard throughout my time at DU, and afterwards, was, "What else can I do to help?" These are the citizen conservationists that make sure healthy ecosystems will be here for future generations. I hope those in my family that follow me will ensure the health of the gifts given freely by our Creator and understand the responsibility we each bear to pass them on to those yet to be born. I am confident they will.

The years at Ducks Unlimited also brought with it wonderful changes in our family life, as well as sadness. In 2012, Erin married the Emergency Room physician she met while on her "Travelling Nurse" assignment and what started out as a 13-week experience ended up with California getting a permanent resident. Eric and Erin wanted to have children right away, and just under a year later, Caleb Sandor Hegedus was born. That same year, Adam met the love of his life in Maryland, and Jaime Thompson, with her beautiful young daughter, Felicity, became part of the family. From the very beginning, Adam treated Felicity as his daughter, and we were pleased to have a ready-made granddaughter join us. Being a father has very little to do with bloodline. It has to do with love and acceptance of responsibility, sometimes when it is not required. Adam has his daughter, and Felicity is the true winner.

On January 29, 2015, Erin and Eric blessed the world with a beautiful girl, Sienna Paige Hegedus. Both Caleb and Sienna were given their parents' middle names, a gesture I thought was quite inventive. I had begun calling Caleb "C-Man" from the day he was born, and when Sienna began to talk, she insisted that I call her "Si-Girl."

I offered several alternatives, but the competition between these two was innate and strong! It's hard to explain to someone who doesn't have children, and especially grandchildren, how tight the emotional bond is with kids who have their own personalities, individual likes and dislikes, and the wonder of life their sponge of a brain can bring to the conversation. I told our children that grandchildren are God's gift to us for putting up with them! That is truer than we care to admit.

Emily graduated from LSU, took a couple of years off, and returned to her pursuit of a law degree. Of all our children, Emily knew what she wanted to do for a living and never changed course. When she got a degree in English, I asked her how she planned to use it.

"It is perfect for becoming a lawyer."

And she did. After graduating from LSU and Loyola of New Orleans School of Law, she remained in New Orleans to practice. I retired from the Fish and Wildlife Service on January 3, 2009. Twelve years later, in January 2021, Emily changed jobs and began her career with the Department of the Interior as an attorney in the Solicitor's office in Atlanta. As a twist of fate, this office of the Solicitor is the same office that provided legal assistance to Sam, me, and the southeast region when I was the Deputy Regional Director. I could not be more proud.

When Sienna was born on January 29th (also the 78th anniversary of Ducks Unlimited), Nell was showing significant signs of deteriorating health. She had to have colon surgery and was less than pleased that she had to have a colostomy. Herman left us 20 years earlier and Nell had no desire to remarry. As her health worsened, so did her drive. Nell was a fighter her whole life and endured thyroid surgery, double mastectomy, hip replacement, knee replacement, and colon cancer. Her tenacious attitude kept her going until she could no longer drive a car and get around on her own.

Melvin had divorced and was a godsend to stay with her and be the caregiver Sarah, Fernell, nor Phyllis could be, given the geographic separation. By 2016, Nell's health was steadily declining, and Erin was afraid Nell would not get to see her new great-granddaughter. A trip to Bunkie by the Hegedus clan was planned for Easter 2016. It was an excellent opportunity for the family to get together and show Nell the wonderful goodness she had produced. Sarah and I joined Emily, Adam, Melvin, Fernell, Richard, and several of the grandchildren at Nell's for a crawfish boil. Phyllis, Sarah's sister and my adopted little sister, and my brother-in-law, Tom Eckerdt, were not able to make it. In Louisiana, a crawfish boil is much more than a meal; it's a social gathering. It was a wonderful celebration, and Nell truly enjoyed it.

Nell Reed, 2016

Just a few months earlier, in October 2015, Melvin and the family received a wonderful surprise when he learned he had an adult daughter! Jalyn Plaisance was suspicious of her true father's identity because of her eye color and dove into a genealogy search. She tracked down an unsuspecting Melvin and asked if they could meet. As soon as he saw Jalyn, he said, "We don't need any tests. You are my daughter."

They both cried, and we gained a wonderful niece. Nell was able to spend time with Jalyn and her surprise great-grandson, Cohen, up until and including the Easter gathering.

On April 13, we lost Nell. She had become my second mother, and I loved her with all my heart. When Richard, Tom, and I went in to tell her goodbye just before she was moved to hospice and put under heavy sedation, she opened her eyes to look at us. We were among a continuous line of quick visits by family members. She knew this was the end. Richard, Tom, and I were all very close to Nell, and she treated us as sons.

"How are you, Nell?" I asked.

"I'd be fine if you all would leave me alone and let me get to sleep!" she replied, then she smiled.

I said, "I love you, Nell."

"I love you more," was her reply. Those were our last words to each other. I was never able to say goodbye to my real mother, but I was blessed to have two and was able to say goodbye to my second.

The two final honors of my career were both associated with my wonderful alma mater, Louisiana State University (LSU). I was sitting in my office in late October 2018 at DU headquarters in Memphis, when my Executive Assistant came into my office and said they needed me in the reception area of the building to have my photo taken with one of our employees who was retiring soon. It was a standing order that when I was needed to congratulate one of our employees or volunteers, it took precedent, and I was to be immediately notified. I made sure each one was offered the opportunity to come into my office and have their photo taken while sitting in the CEO's chair. I believed it was their chair and I was simply honored to occupy it.

When I went up front to have the photo taken, I was surprised by a group of people, one of which was Sarah, and another was Cliff Vannoy, President and CEO of the LSU Alumni Association. Cliff was decked out in a full tuxedo and had a poster on an easel stand that had my name, photo, and announcement that I had been selected as the 2019 LSU Alumnus of the Year! I was so caught off guard that I just froze. Everyone, especially Sarah, really enjoyed seeing me "speechless."

Cliff let me know that following my induction into the LSU School of Renewable Natural Resources Hall of Fame the prior year, the Alumni Association had begun to look at my career. Dr. Luke Laborde of the LSU School of RNR and a DU volunteer had apparently written the nomination to the Alumni board, and I had been selected. After all LSU had done for me in my early life, to include giving me a *new* life, this was overwhelming. On April 5, 2019, the formal induction into the LSU Hall of Distinction took place, and I was surrounded by over two dozen family members and wonderful friends. It was a black-tie affair and one that will remain a treasured memory for as long as I live.

One of the joys I was able to experience was when I told the story of how I had been left adrift by Eastern Kentucky University, and Fred Bryan had stepped up and given me a new start. I was able to have Fred stand and be recognized by the entire audience. It was inadequate for all he had done, but I could tell he truly appreciated my making him part of my evening. Later that fall during homecoming weekend, Sarah and I rode in the homecoming parade and attended the LSU v. Florida football game. Not only did LSU win that game, but they also went on to have an undefeated season and win the national championship! To be the alumnus of the year when the LSU Tigers went undefeated was more than I could have hoped for. Little did I know there would be more.

L–R: Adam, Sarah, Dale, Erin, Emily at LSU Induction, April 2019

The second surprise came in the late spring of 2021 when I received a call from Dr. Luke Laborde asking me if I would agree to let LSU and Ducks Unlimited establish an endowed professorship in my name.

"What? You're asking me if I would *mind*?"

After stuttering for a moment, I said it would be an honor and privilege to have the "H. Dale Hall-Ducks Unlimited Endowed Professorship in Wetlands and Waterfowl Conservation at Louisiana State University" created in my honor. Very few people have endowed professorships established without making significant financial contributions, and this kid from Harlan County, Kentucky was just asked if one could be done in his name. No words can adequately describe the humbling emotions that flood your senses when something like this occurs. Outside my marriage and the birth of my children and grandchildren, nothing can compare. I offer no argument that I in any way deserved these honors that LSU and DU had bestowed upon me. There are so many others that are more deserving. The only words that come to mind, though woefully inadequate, are, "THANK YOU."

As I finished my time at DU and began writing COMPELLED, the story of my career, I was reminded of all the times in my life that my Creator's hand was guiding and watching over me. For those who don't believe in divine intervention, I respectfully say I cannot find any analysis, scientific or otherwise, that does *not* lead to the conclusion of a Creator. Stephen Hawking, the renowned cosmologist, once performed an evaluation going back in time to the "big bang" when an infinitesimal black hole was preparing to explode. When he reached that stage, he said there was only "singularity" and, therefore, there was no God. As a scientist, my next question is, "Then who created singularity?"

No matter how one approaches spirituality and creation, whether it is the string theory multiverse or ancient aliens that occupied (or still occupy) earth, there is still the question of, "Who created them?" I don't propose to know the answer as to who or what the Creator is, but I know deep in my soul that a power has guided me throughout my life, and I owe that power my love, trust, and allegiance. That's good enough for me.

In July 2019, I began opening the forty or more boxes of files, memoranda, court decisions, and other papers documenting both my journey and what was happening during my lifetime. I segregated the material dealing mostly with my family life and incorporated it into this book. The materials dealing with my professional career and the evolution of natural resource conservation in the U.S. were covered in COMPELLED, *From the Yazoo Pumps to polar bears and back, the evolution of natural resource conservation and law.*

That book was published in July 2022, and I allowed Ducks Unlimited to sell the book for me and keep all profits, to be directed to the LSU endowed professorship.

Bass Pro Shops and my good friend, Johnny Morris, also purchased books and have them for sale online. At this writing, Bass Pro has already made a donation to the endowed chair in excess of the profits of the first 2,000 books they purchased. As is true with Johnny Morris in all things, I know this is only the beginning. I have reserved 100% of the rights to the book and may well allow others to sell it later, as well as possibly in digital form. But for the first few years, it is only fitting that the university that saved me, the company that inspired me to create the term "citizen conservationist," and the conservation community that represents all the good in mankind should be the first to benefit from *their* story.

The journey I traveled from Appalachia to Memphis has been guided by the hand of my Creator, sometimes with a swift kick in the rear to get my attention, and I know I would be nothing without the angel he sent to walk with me. I have truly been blessed in my life and will continue to do all I can to help others come to appreciate the artful beauty our Creator has painted all around us. My fervent desire is that generations to follow will judge us kindly, with the understanding that we are all students of the universe and prone to make mistakes. But just as the Man in the Arena, we continue to get up, try again, and hopefully become better stewards of the gifts we have been given.

A very popular song written by Darrell Scott and beautifully sung by Patty Loveless is called, "You'll Never Leave Harlan Alive," and tells the story of despair in the coal mines of Harlan County, Kentucky. While I did leave Harlan and pursued a life that has taken me all over the United States, there is no doubt that Harlan never left me. I have always known I was a child from the bosom of the Cumberland Plateau of the Appalachian Mountains. For that, I am eternally grateful.

REFERENCES

Grizzle, Anna Lee. August 27, 2019. Personal Communication.

Lee, Jackie Goshen. August 22, 2019. Personal Communication.

Williams, John. 1975. Personal Communication.

ABOUT THE AUTHOR

H. Dale Hall has over 45 years of professional experience in fish and wildlife resource management in both the federal and private sectors. Following a four-year commitment in the U.S. Air Force, he attended college at Cumberland College, Eastern Kentucky University, and Louisiana State University. He began his career as a wetlands biologist with the U.S. Fish and Wildlife Service in Vicksburg, Mississippi, and retired over thirty years later as the Director, appointed by President George W. Bush and unanimously confirmed by the U.S. Senate. In 2010, Hall became Chief Executive Officer of Ducks Unlimited, Inc. and retired after nine years in that role.

During his career, Hall was recognized as Conservationist of the Year twice; received commendations from the governors of Kentucky, Arkansas, and Tennessee; was inducted into the LSU SNR Hall of Fame and was named the Louisiana State University Alumnus of the Year in 2019. He is author of *Compelled: From the Yazoo Pumps to Polar Bears and Back; The Evolution of Natural Resource Conservation and Law*. He can be reached at hdalehallllc@gmail.com, or on Facebook at H. Dale Hall, LLC.

www.ingramcontent.com/pod-product-compliance
Lightning Source LLC
Chambersburg PA
CBHW071116160426
43196CB00013B/2590